That Ye Might Have

Part Two of

A Trilogy

Part One – I Came
Part Two – That Ye Might Have
Part Three – Life More Abundant

Other Writings by Walter Lanyon

2 A. M. ◆ Abd Allah, Teacher, Healer
And It Was Told of a Certain Potter
Behold the Man ◆ Demonstration
Embers ◆ The Eyes of the Blind
I Came ◆ The Impatient Dawn
Impressions of a Nomad
It Is Wonderful ◆ The Joy Bringer
A Lamp unto My Feet
The Laughter of God ◆ Leaves of the Tree
A Light Set upon a Hill
Life More Abundant
London Notes and Lectures
Out of the Clouds
Quintology: Ask and Ye Shall Receive
A Royal Diadem
The Temple Not Made with Hands
Thrust in the Sickle ◆ Treatment
Without the Smell of Fire
Your Heritage

Available through:
Mystics of the World
Eliot, Maine
www.mysticsoftheworld.com

That Ye Might Have

Part Two of

A Trilogy

Walter Lanyon

Part One – I Came
Part Two – That Ye Might Have
Part Three – Life More Abundant

That Ye Might Have

Mystics of the World First Edition 2014
Published by Mystics of the World
ISBN-13: 978-0692350409
ISBN-10: 0692350403

> For information contact:
> Mystics of the World
> Eliot, Maine
> www.mysticsoftheworld.com

Cover graphics by Margra Muirhead
Printed by CreateSpace
Available from Mystics of the World and Amazon.com

∽ ∼

Walter C. Lanyon, 1887 – 1967
Originally published 1940

Contents

Chapter I
   The Hall of Silence 9
Chapter II
   Substance 21
Chapter III
   Idle Gossip Sinks Ships 34
Chapter IV
   The Spreading Dawn 40
Chapter V
   The God of Love 64
Chapter VI
   Direct Action 69
Chapter VII
   Reincarnation and You 81
Chapter VIII
   The Day of Miracles 93
Chapter IX
   White Elephants 99
Chapter X
   The Inspiration 107
Chapter XI
   Experience—and Straightway the Spirit 115
Chapter XII
   Let No Man Deceive You 122
Chapter XIII
   No Competition 127

Chapter XIV
　No Weapon Shall Prosper 136
Chapter XV
　If Any Man..145
Chapter XVI
　The Permanent Identity 157
Chapter XVII
　Evolution and God 167
Chapter XVIII
　But Why Should This Happen to Me?.....................170
Chapter XIX
　Nothing Hidden..175
Chapter XX
　The Year of Our Lord 179
Chapter XXI
　I Will Not Let You Go 181
Chapter XXII
　Hid with Christ in God 188
Chapter XXIII
　Between Two Opinions How Long Halt Ye?.........190
Chapter XXIV
　Symbols...196
Meditations
　Not a Sparrow Falleth 202
　Adultery..205
　Preparation 207
　The Gods Give Thread 209
　Fire and Duck 210
Notes...211
About the Author 215

The Child finds its mother when it leaves her womb. When I am parted from you, thrown out from your household, I am free to see your face. … I walk my own willful way till my very folly tempts you to my door. For I have your promise that my portion of the best in this world will come from your hands.

—Rabindranath Tagore

Do you hear? Do you begin to see that we are the sons of God merging into the Fatherhood degree and that we have a right to the kingdom of heaven here and now and a right to offset all the times that evil has seemed to triumph over God? "Who is so great a God as our God?"
—Walter Lanyon

Chapter I

The Hall of Silence

*I go to prepare a place for you ...
that where I am, there ye may be also.*

The place that is prepared is the Hall of Silence in the Temple of Peace. It is more than the "closet" referred to so often, for in this Hall of Silence, the completed and perfect thing is visible ere it goes down through the temple of your body to take on a material form and shape. It becomes an actual place of experience, a laboratory.

Shamballa, Shangri La, even Tibet (as far as it is anything to you) are merely states of consciousness, all of them attainable by you and leading many times to bringing out a materialization of these places. I cannot understand why, if your mind can go to such places, your body should not accompany it—especially if you have experienced the union of body and Soul, God and man. Do you see why, when you have chosen the *alone* path, you are free to go just as fast as you wish, free to "call upon Me" and to know and experience the sustaining Principle in direct proportion to your acceptance?

"He shall prepare a table before me in the presence of mine enemies." Quite a lovely promise. Is it any good? Can you avail yourself of it? If not, why not?

Coming to this consciousness, there are:

> "No contortions and twistings of the body in Yoga practices. No hundreds of mantras each day, repeated monotonously; no turning of prayer wheels! Just a simplicity of Nature—like the birds, the bees, and the flowers. Just a natural and sweet return to God."

And so you, standing in the Hall of Silence in the Temple of Peace, are able to travel out through the Light to reach the consciousness which is calling unto you on his level of understanding and to stimulate you to drink deeper of the Truth. And as the color or order of his coming intensifies, it finally reaches the great white Light of Self-revelation.

Silence is the first sign of real wisdom. Any real spiritual experience is too sacred to be profaned by words. Do you see why? You can give it all to the world and keep it all, but you cannot tell a thing you have experienced in the Hall of Silence lest you find the door closed to you. "Then went he in and shut the door." And what happened? And what will happen to you when you have, like the Arab, "silently stolen away" into this Hall of Silence and discovered the secret pattern—the matrix, the model of that which is about to appear on the earth? It is too sacred to set down on paper that which is to be shown to you—how it is that you can perform the whole thing in the place of Consciousness and send it forth to take on a body and form.

There is no limit to what can be accomplished through completing the recognition in the Place of Silence. Even a surgical operation, no matter how difficult, could be perfectly consummated and finished so that the light passing through the various degrees could guide the hands of the one actually performing it in the operating room. And too, an operation could be so perfectly done that it would pass through into manifestation without the aid of outside hands. Do you begin to see how Jesus "went unto his Father" and accomplished His miracles before the light was stepped down from the Hall of Silence into actual embodiment in the flesh?

All this I write to you from the plane of revelation; *you* must read between the lines.

In this Hall of Silence, which is within your consciousness, do you find the secret, and you can release it in whatever form necessary. All this seems strange and vague, perhaps a little foolish, as I write the words (all the wisdom of God is foolishness in the eyes of man), and yet *you* will understand—a real, secret laboratory of the soul, which you will boldly enter and possess. "Come boldly to the throne of grace," for now you come not *to get* but *to let* the light flow from the throne of God, straight through the human temple of you, into expression.

"My sheep hear my voice." Do you?

"Put thou a seal upon my lips."

"Thou fool, do you not know that a seed must first fall into the ground and rot before it shall be made alive?" And it means just that.

Silence is absolutely necessary for the germination of any new idea, just as it is for the seed. It lies in the secret, silent place, in the darkness, hid from the prying eyes of human thought that, with all its science and intellect, has not yet discovered just what it is that brings about the miracle of birth. You are told to, "Tell no man." "Show John." But if you find you know better than Jesus did, or does, then you must uncover every wonderful thing and expose it to the curious minds of unbelief and bring forth a stillborn.

"See that ye tell no man." That is a hard task for the old talking human thought. It wants to tell everything it hears, knows, or even suspects; but the moment a thing is told, it begins to lose power, just as the moment a valve is opened, an engine loses steam. The thing that is held in secrecy within you gains momentum—builds its body in silence and is protected from the curious, unbelieving thought.

If you are an invalid and have been one for years, no one believes you are going to be healed. They may be charitable enough to want you to be well (I am not too awfully sure of this, but let us be generous and say they do), but one thing is sure—they don't believe it. You are just another of those "poor things" who are so much to be pitied.

I once heard a lady talking about how she was going to be rich. She seemed almost inspired. She told the entire law of how it was taking place, what she had learned, and how she was going to gain her wealth through demonstration. As she talked, the crowd gathered, half-carried away with the fervor of her words. Then all of a sudden something happened, the same thing that happens to champagne when it stands uncorked too long. Suddenly everybody seemed to feel that she was just talking, and they began to titter; and she went on baring her very soul until it became almost shameful. She never got rich, and finally she had to turn corners to avoid meeting some of her former listeners, who always greeted her with, "Well, have the riches come yet?"

I think you will find that in this spiritual progress Jesus knew exactly what He was talking about when He said, "Tell nothing," and that advice must be followed if anything is to be brought into manifestation.

Magnifying the power of God within you until it actually *becomes* you is the way of automatic expression. The trained athlete does not have to force his expression of strength. A baby may have to push with all his might and main to move a ball from the table, while an athlete may brush aside an obstacle which would cause other men to put forth great effort. Why? Because of the consciousness of strength and power within. It has become effortless because he is aware of the power within his body-temple.

While this illustration is a poor picture compared with the Power within you, which can and will do the "impossible" even through your weakness, yet it will give you something of the feel of what is meant by the prayer "Be still, and know that I am God"—that the very I AM within you is God in essence and is only awaiting the opportunity of expression. It only needs to be recognized. Saying, "I recognize the power of God within me," does no more for you than saying, "I am rich," will do to a poor man and will only bring the derision of the crowd upon your head. But becoming conscious of God in the midst of you is another story, and this is only done by silence and secrecy.

Every time the secret is told, you are deprived of the manifestation and must go again the rounds of preparing the ground and planting the seed, and you will continue this monotonous repetition until you put the seal upon your lips and magnify the power of the Lord within you.

I know people may talk and wonder what you are doing, and they may offer advice and help; but just wait. A day will come, perhaps much sooner than you think—a day wherein you have filled the chalice of your consciousness with God to the brim, and then, "All shall be changed in the twinkling," and you can *show*. The mystery of this lovely working of

Power within you is that which brings forth the Light.

You are also told in this lesson of secrecy to "salute no man" you pass on the highway of life, because he is just the one to open up all the valves of the engine and let out all the steam. And when the boiler is cold and empty, the one "whose breath is in his nostrils" leaves a parting word with you: "Why, of course, my dear, I always knew there was nothing to it." And don't forget that the one whose breath is in his nostrils may attend thousands of lectures on Truth and read every book written on the subject. If the breath has gotten no farther than his nostrils, he only chatters words and ideas and has yet to experience the deep inbreathing of the breath of the Lord.

Little people running about "talking truth" are like so many cottontails bobbing up here and there all over the place, and they want nothing more than a nice head of cabbage for dinner. *I* said to you, "Feed my sheep" — and let the cottontails alone.

Remember, you cannot prove a single word of Jesus Christ just to satisfy the curiosity of a human mind. The immovable nature of the law makes it imperative that you come up to it before it apparently comes down to you. As you merge into this Presence, you are less and less concerned about the *spreading* of truth and more and more interested in the *letting* of the light so shine before men.

The red flag of danger is waved in your face when it comes to talking. *Flee* from the short-lived, human, inbreathed thing "whose breath is in his nostrils." Do you begin to see the difference in the awakened soul and the one who is still wandering in a dream of evil? One has his breath in his nostrils; it has not yet gone deeper. He is capable of all evil and only evil, no matter what amount of "good" he apparently accomplishes for the moment. The other is inbreathed with the breath of Life. He has become a Living Soul, which cannot and does not die. Do you begin to see that when you are inbreathed with the breath of Life, you are for the first time at the portals of immortality?

"Flee"—it is a sudden warning and danger signal. Don't tell a thing. Agree with him instantly, even if he says there is no God, for that is true to him, and you are only agreeing with his state of mind. "Agree with thine adversary," the short-breathed thing which knows evil and denies, even when he is acknowledging God. The agreement with his evil will give him the chance of handling it in his own way.

"Let the earth keep silent before Me and renew her strength." If your earth, or body, has been all shot to pieces by the years of talking of and about the Truth, presently you will feel the great soft folds of silence enveloping you. And presently you will feel the renewing of your earth-body and affairs. The Power is as gentle as the shepherd leading "those that are with young." You are with young, a

The Hall of Silence

great flock of new and lovely ideas which are to be brought out, but you must stay out of the highways and byways of human thought and talk. You can do this, even while you are apparently in the midst of it, by placing the Seal upon your lips.

So many souls awaken in the midst of such bedlam that it seems almost hopeless to extricate themselves. Fighting, arguing, and beating against circumstances will do nothing. Presently, in the deep place of secrecy is found the place of recognition. On the outside, the whirl of evil continues, but it receives no more life-substance from you; you are judging not from appearances, but righteous judgment, and are magnifying in silence "these things in your heart." And then one day, perhaps the very next, the door is suddenly sprung open, and you go free into the new day of expression.

Silence is the first indication of real understanding. People who know the deep mysteries do not talk about them. Can you imagine Jesus advertising all sorts of new ideas and tricks to be given at His next talk? Can you see that the more and larger the benefits advertised, the farther the whole thing is from the truth of Jesus Christ? "The fame of him went abroad" over all Israel. There were no radios, loud speakers, or amplifiers (the still small voice does not need to be amplified); no newspapers, no cinemas, no "believe-it-or-nots." There was just what? Just the same thing which is at this moment welling up in you. There was, and is, just God, waiting for the opportunity to express through you. When He knows, then the world knows; so, "See that you tell no man." The fame of you (if necessary) will go abroad in all Israel. You cannot fail on this secret mission because that which is known of God is known of man as manifestation, and that which you tell in secret shall be called from the housetops.

It is wonderful and glorious, this sudden coming into the place of secrecy and silence. "Keep silent before Me." And presently you will "stand upon your watch and see what the Spirit has to say unto you." It has plenty to say unto you. It has the plan for the Father's business, which is to be carried out through your temple.

This secrecy does not imply a withdrawing from the world or from people. "In the world, but not of it." In the midst of the most noisy turmoil yet not of it or far away from it all. This secrecy does not make you strange and different, but it makes you unconsciously powerful, and you will have this verified at the strangest moments of your on-going. Someone will "see the Light" in you and put it into some kind of words, a little acknowledgment along the highway of Life.

Note how it was that Jesus never helped or healed anyone unless they came first to Him and acknowledged the God within Him, and then He spoke freely what the Spirit had to say unto that individual. You remember, too, that "you need but open your mouth; *I* will supply the words"—will give you the exact or unique word of help or releasement to say to the one who is asking. But be sure they are asking.

Once you are over the first hurdle of holding your tongue and keeping *within* the good things you know, there will come a positive joy in the new secrecy which possesses you. You will listen and listen and listen—and my, oh my, what you will hear! And presently you will begin to "hear" something as you listen, and it will enable you to diagnose everything that comes to you without difficulty.

When the boiler can hold no more steam and the pressure has reached its maximum, then something has got to take place. So keep every valve closed. Don't tell anyone, not even your spiritual adviser, about the deep and lovely desires and secrets that are within your soul. *No one is safe with the Annunciation message but you, so keep it locked within your soul.* You have much to accomplish before it comes into manifestation but nothing that cannot take place easily and naturally if you have kept silent. As you wait upon Me, sometimes the old human mind gets excited and worried, but the Voice within says, "The time is not yet ... Be still, and know that I am God"; and again you magnify the Power and wait in the holy Silence with this glorious assurance in you, "It is done." It is gathering a body together for expression.

Nothing can come through the confusion of human thinking, because the moment an idea is placed on earth, the Herod-thought tries to kill it. The human thought will kill every "male child" you try to bring to earth. So don't be a "wise man" and tell where the event is to take place. Keep silent before Me.

Did you ever think of what great trouble the wise men actually caused because they ran about telling of things to come? Two thousand children were killed as a result of it. I imagine it was time for them to leave town after starting that sort of thing, don't you? Don't be a "wise man" literally; and yet symbolically you are the wise man and see the lovely star in the East that leads you to the very spot where your manifestation is taking place, and that spot is *within you*. How wonderful it all is, so filled with glory and light and so fraught with power.

So are you cloaked in silence and secrecy, knowing that when you speak, you speak no longer of yourself but "of him that sent me" into expression. When you are thus speaking, you are speaking in the first person and the present tense; otherwise you are speaking of and about truth, either past or future, and nothing happens. When you speak the Word of God, it does not return unto you void but does accomplish whereunto it is sent; but when you speak the words of man, they scatter like the host of troubles released from the Pandora box and bring only evil to you.

"Put thou a seal upon my lips."

Chapter II

Substance

An eager student of Truth once went to India to study the ways of the Far East under a great teacher, who was reputed to hold Truth above everything else in the world.

Having whole-heartedly accepted the world's dictum that poverty and asceticism must go hand in hand with spirituality, the student had long since taken the vow of poverty. What was his horror to find the master, not sitting in a loincloth under a banyan tree, but living in ease and comfort in a marble palace, surrounded by treasures that beggared the splendors of the *Arabian Nights*. Further, the master was beautifully dressed, in Oriental fashion, and wore magnificent jewels.

The student was unable to restrain his amazement and spoke at some length of his views on the fleshpots of Egypt and the uselessness of material possessions. The master sat quietly by on his luxurious divan, waiting for the student to finish his tirade against riches, luxury, and worldly goods. And then he spoke: "It is not the possession *of* things, but the possession by them that counts. I have no interest in things for their worldly value, but for the beauty and comfort they give me."

This did not please the young student, who argued that if the master had no interest in them, he should renounce them all. Even while he spoke, an alarm of fire was heard in the palace, and through the wide-open portals of the spacious rooms could be seen the flames, hungrily devouring all the precious works of art. As the master seemed quite unperturbed, the student jumped into action, shouting frantic orders to the servants as to how the furnishings and art treasures should be saved.

The teacher sat quietly by. The student rushed over to him. "Get up and help. All these wonderful and valuable things are being destroyed." But still the teacher sat and smiled. Finally, worn out with his efforts, the breathless student once more implored the master, "For the love of God, do something to save all this wealth," and the teacher answered, "I am not concerned. I possess it now and can always replace it, but as wealth it has no value to me. Yet you, who have come all this way to tell me how you have renounced wealth, are in a terrible state of excitement and rage over the destruction of that which you have repeatedly told me was nothing." Then, as the astounded student looked about him, he saw that the fire had receded and had left no trace of damage.

There is a difference in possessing things and being possessed by them—and so watch out that your condemnation of money and wealth is not motivated by the sad knowledge that you cannot attract it.

Substance

Many people who claim that "things do not matter" only say so because they cannot get things. And many a person has taken the poverty vow because he already had so much poverty in his life that he knew nothing else to worship.

As long as you have to have a chair, it might just as well be the type and kind which pleases you most. The value being put on it by man makes it valueless to God. I have seen the chair that a so-called famous personage sat in raised to such value that one could have bought perhaps a thousand chairs of the same make and age for the price. And the bed of a French Court favorite has brought such a fabulous price that it was fantastic; yet the bed and the chair were comparatively worthless in materials. The only value was that placed on them by man. Rosewood is burned for firewood in some parts of the world, and yet rosewood in some places is very valuable.

Do you begin to see how it is that before any sense of substance can come through to you the value of things must be taken away from them? This does not imply disrespect for works of art or even things for everyday use, but it breaks down one of the great barriers between you and the manifestation. Do you possess things, or do they possess you?

The apparent failure of prayers for substance is due to the fact that man has mistakenly placed the idea of substance in the thing instead of in what is back of it. The substance is not in the symbol of money but in what is back of it, as has been so clearly demonstrated by the various inflations and failures of monetary systems. It is a big step towards the possession of substance when the *love* of things and money is taken away. Then nothing is found to be wrong with the money or things, and the recognition of the primal substance is placed in God instead of in the shadow of matter cast for the moment into expression. Feathers and beads were given in exchange for much land, yet of what value are those feathers and beads today?

Are you fooled in your understanding of the Truth to the extent that you say one thing with your lips and feel another with your heart? I often hear people say, "I want no money except for the bare necessities of life." That is subterfuge. If you don't believe it, while that one is talking, drop a dime on the pavement and see what happens! If you don't want money in a land where money is absolutely essential for the convenience of exchange, it is time you checked on your honesty of purpose. Don't fool yourself in wanting to serve the world when you cannot serve yourself.

Do you begin to understand why the Master has given such strict and meager — yet elaborate — instructions for it all? "He that hath eyes, let *him* see what the scriptures say unto the churches (temple-bodies)." What the scriptures say unto your church-body is for you and only for you, and through this temple service are you able to "let your light so shine," that there will be "enough and to spare" of everything necessary for you to carry on the expression of the John Smith incarnation you have taken on at this time.

Until you can see this "substance of things hoped for and the evidence of things not yet seen," you can expect few and small financial returns from affirmations and from following organizational instructions of how to "get what you want."

The handwriting on the wall is plain. When you begin to watch with the single eye, you will detect the spurious from the true. Jesus offered no courses in how to get health, wealth, and happiness in twenty-five lessons for so many dollars. He held no secret key to the Truth for which He charged a price. He made it especially clear that no man had a special dispensation or enjoyed any preferred rights that all men did not have the same opportunity to appropriate.

There is only one mediator, remember. Location has nothing to do with God, and so He is as much present in the worst sump hole of so-called iniquity as He is on the most lofty mountain or temple dedicated to Him. <u>If God is all-present, He is—or else He isn't.</u> "Choose ye this day whom you will serve," for when you serve God, "He will give you (not you and some secret method or group, but *you*) the desires of your heart." It says the desires of *your* heart, and it does not qualify those desires; and it also says that windows will be opened in heaven (your consciousness) and blessings will be poured out to such an extent that you cannot receive them.

The John Smith incarnation has never dreamed of such things; in fact, he cannot think of it because it is not possible on the three-dimensional plane of his thinking. But nevertheless, it is so and it is true.

Once the old idea of "demonstrating" money is destroyed in you, you will see that substance is as natural and normal as anything else in life. Your breathing is natural and normal until you get the human thought in the way of it, and then it becomes congested and produces a stoppage.

So is it with substance. The impossible becomes the possible when you stop trying to make it happen and find it natural. The going unto the Father, the blending into the *Oneness* of God, the recognition of your Permanent Identity—all these things bring you to understand that substance is natural and real and is not at the beck and call of human thought.

A woman told me she had "worked" as a practitioner for God for twenty years, and yet she did not have carfare home. She was worthy, and she was apparently honest, but the fly in the ointment was that she imagined she had been working for God when she collected all fees and lived from them; and also when she wondered (of course, as she explained, it was none of her business, nor was she criticizing) how her friend, who did not work for God but lived joyously and happily, could have everything and live a life of silken dalliance.

Well, the harder you "work" for money, the poorer you get; and the more you stop "working" for money, the greater the possibility of the Life element functioning through your temple-being. It is all contrary to your course of twenty-five lessons for twenty-five dollars—but everything in God's kingdom is contrary to the laws of man for the simple reason that "the wisdom of man (and that includes your twenty-five lessons at twenty-five dollars) is foolishness in the eyes of God."

If it is all foolishness, then what can you expect to do about it? And will you find yourself caught in the same false equation in which the student in India found himself—saying one thing but believing another? "As a man thinketh (feels) in his heart, so is he."

How do you *feel* about money, anyway? Don't tell me—tell yourself; perhaps you will be surprised at what you hear.

Of course, at the heart of the love of money is the fear that something might cut things off for you and that you would eventually die for want of bread. This fear is backed up by plenty of tangible evidence; there are plenty of appearances to justify the fear. That is why Jesus said, "He that loseth his life shall find it." He that loses his individual, separate life shall find the universal Life, which is not at any time deprived of Its manifestation. *It is only the thought of separation which causes the idea of lack to manifest in the world of matter.*

The contemplation of Oneness fills you with light and devitalizes all fear of lack. Arising from this "touch" with Oneness, this recognition of the All causes man to experience the manifestation of substance in whatever degree he can take it. There are thousands of degrees of substance, and what is wealth to one is poverty to another; yet it makes no difference about that. Your degree is your own; and if it is not large enough to meet the needs amply and beautifully, it is time for you to push out from the shores of your former limitations, to "launch out onto the deeper waters," to "enlarge the borders of your tent."

Such a wonderful new vista opens before the individual when he even touches the *Oneness* of Life. He begins to sense-feel dimensions of God which cannot be easily set down in black and white. He looks again and sees things taking place which *cannot* happen—and by a way which is natural and normal instead of supernatural, as it was in the days of waiting for miracles or magic to happen.

It is recorded that their clothes "waxed not old" nor their shoes, etc., and they had been using them for forty years. See anything in this? How does it fit in with the law of friction, deterioration, age, and all the rest of the man-science laws? Just cannot be, can it? Well, of course not. You have never seen it happen, and no man can prove it, so it must be foolishness; and so it *is* in the eyes of man. But why in heaven's name will that very same man try to "demonstrate" money or jobs or health, since they are all quite as impossible.

Remember too that just because you have never seen a thing done does not mean that it cannot be done; and also that you will never see it done as long as you indulge in any curiosity, for curiosity is merely disbelief which hopes to get by and "peep" into the Holy of Holies.

Remember, there are "no peepers allowed" in the kingdom of heaven, for nothing is going to profane the works and the powers of God. "All power is given unto me," and when you begin to sense this "Look again, the fields are white," you will also begin to understand why the grain of mustard can also do the works, and so on down the line of Life.

You have been told that a rich man cannot enter the kingdom of heaven and have misunderstood this to mean a man with many possessions; yet it could mean a man possessed of the *love* of money, while yet wanting for love of anything else. It is merely an attempt to show you that the worship of anything other than God is one of the ways to keep you out of this consciousness of ease and substance. The rich man referred to may be rich in many things—that is, he may have an abundance of evil in his soul, or judging, condemning, criticizing, and the like—and he may also have a large bank account. But the rich man is many times the poor man when it comes to actual dollars and cents. The "rich young man" could not let go of his worship of money as a power apart from God, hence, he could not enter in, for he depended on things and not on God.

Do you begin to see how it is that the value placed on money is what keeps it away from you, and how it is that the "trying" to demonstrate it only puts you in the power of the gods of man's creating? Money is the chief god of this thought-taking world, and if you fall down and worship this god, you must commit your ways unto him and be directed by him in order to attain money. When a person sets out to demonstrate a fortune, he immediately runs into the battle with the gods of this world, and naturally he is going to be defeated.

"Render unto Caesar the things that are Caesar's." Do you begin to understand a little of the laws of substance?

"You shall ask whatsoever you will, and it shall be done unto you." That is a pretty large order, but it is true. Your "whatsoever" is what *you* ask for, and that is all you can get, no matter how much another takes by the same asking. "Awake thou that sleepest, and Christ shall give thee light." Awake and arise from the dead!

The vacuum created by human want increases until it fills all space in the human thinking and brings with it the manifestation of this thought. The vacuum created by the belief in lack with the five thousand was as real to Jesus as it was to any of the men. He recognized their law of hunger and lack and fatigue. He said something to the effect that they had been three days without bread, etc. But notice what happened. "Then lifted he his eyes to heaven and gave thanks." We see Him, right before their eyes, blending with the *One* and giving thanks for the Presence, and instantly there was the inrush of Substance that filled the vacuum of human thinking. In a little while the belief in hunger was gone, and a surplus left of twelve hampers of scraps!

I mention these twelve hampers because they should have been sizeable—and where did they come from? Ever think about all the things that are sandwiched in between the lines of the Bible for those who have "eyes"? The manifestation of twelve hampers to hold so much bread would be a man-sized job in itself and quite as wonderful as the production of bread and fishes!

The wonder of it all was to happen the next morning, when they came to Him again for bread and He said to them, "You seek me for the bread, but you cannot find me. Did you not see the miracle?" In other words, did you not "get on" to the working of the law of Christ Jesus and would therefore be able to do the same thing yourself? And this surprised question was addressed not only to His disciples and especially close followers but also to the simple man in the street, indicating that all could have done the same thing if they had so much as glimpsed the law.

Isn't it wonderful how simple it all was to Jesus, and isn't it revealing to you to note the surprise He always expressed that the man in the street did not follow His example after being shown the way. Well, it is enough to make your heart burn within you to know that we are now approaching the wonderful revelation of Jesus Christ, even though it has been two thousand years.

The point of attack with Jesus seemed to be, "None of these things (appearances) move me." Not any of them. That was His first reaction. He simply was not affected by appearances. He did not demonstrate over them—He did not recognize them. He moved into the next dimension of Life, where the things of the lesser dimension had no power or reality, and invited you to do the same thing, saying that it was all possible to a *child*.

Yes, it is necessary to go over and over the wonder of it all and to note from time to time that you were created (not born) a little lower than the angels and given dominion over everything on, over, and under the earth, skies, and waters. That's the fact of your case, and the sooner you hark back to that place of Power, the sooner you will find many of the "inventions and creations" of mankind fading into the nothingness of yesterday. The sooner you make your assumption of your oneness with God as something more than an affirmation of truth, you will change the face of many things, remembering all the while that you were given dominion over everything—and that means *everything*.

What say you? Do you begin to understand how it is that the little symbol of money, which today is and tomorrow is not, cannot control you or regulate your life or stop your life from its functioning, as long as you are "<u>hid with Christ (your consciousness) in God</u>"?

>"He openeth his hand
>and satisfieth the desire
>of every living thing."

>Do you hear?

Chapter III

Idle Gossip Sinks Ships

I received a letter today. The information printed on the envelope by the U. S. Government sounded not unlike some of the words of Jesus Christ.

And yet you say that words are not powerful! I question the use of *idle* in front of gossip, for in my opinion there is no other kind. But the whole thing tells a story too important to be missed.

The Word of God goes through into manifestation whenever spoken in the *nature* (name) of Jesus Christ, and in like manner, the words of the human mind accomplish their degree of evil with the same apparent ease. The human mind is concerned with words. The Divine has *the Word*, and while to some this may seem a play on words, yet to the one who has "eyes to see," there is something of great import.

Gradually, we are beginning to see that, "as in Christ all shall be made alive, so in Adam all shall die." That is, as in the Word of God all goodness and heaven shall come into being, so by the words of Adam (human thought) all shall die, be killed. "The word of God is quick, and powerful, and sharper than a two-edged sword," and that is why Jesus counseled us to be alert to this Word and to flee from the man who is filled with "words" — opinions, beliefs, gossip, scandal. Do you begin to see what is taking place in the world of words, in the level of human thought?

It is recorded that harlots, thieves, murderers, liars, etc., all go into the kingdom of heaven before the scandalmonger. And that is because it is easier to justify any of those crimes than it is the crime of gossip and scandal. I am sure the scandalmonger who has caused something terrible to happen by his talk has a very difficult job getting into the kingdom of heaven, into the state of Consciousness where contentment and peace abide.

Some time ago a girl returned from the East and brought with her a baby. She said she had been married secretly. Six months afterwards, they found her dead in her home. The doctor could find no apparent cause for her death. Can you?

She had been stoned to death, silently pelted with pity, sympathy, and downright murderous thoughts which she didn't know how to escape. There was a good deal of wailing at the funeral, and it is reported that half a hundred wonderful people came forward and offered to see that the little mite had a good home. But you know how it is. Or do you?

If you are hid with Christ in God, you begin to know that there is no such thing as an illegitimate creation. How could there be? And this is not to condone irregularities in the human code but to prove to you that when the urge of Spirit comes to express Itself in a new temple, It will supply the way and means. And the thought that God's creation has to be stamped "illegitimate" is too grotesque to stand the simple honest light of day.

All of us are illegitimate, for that matter, until we suddenly claim the same Father Jesus had. "Call no man your father." Why? Because if you do, you have all the damning inheritance of the illegitimate son, the bastard. There is the son of the bondwoman and the Son of the Free, and all these things are for you to contemplate.

Many people who profess to believe in the Bible exclaim, "Of course I believe that God is my Father." Well, that changes the whole picture, *if you do*, for in that case you have ceased the inheritance of the Adam affair and have begun to call upon Me, to look unto Me, and to ask of Me; and as surely as the material father would supply you with good gifts, I can much more supply you with the kingdom of heaven.

Do you begin to see how everything that is not born of God is illegitimate and must come under the condemnation of the illegitimate? No wonder that so many things you try to do go wrong; you are stoned too, in one way or another, because of this illegitimacy. All this will reveal itself to you.

We are beginning to see and sense what it is to be born of God. It means we are experiencing in a degree the immaculate conception; we are beginning to "call no man our father" and to look, actually and practically, to God as the source of Life and everything necessary for Life.

All the human patterns differ in various countries. What is sin in one place is not in another, but what is sin in the eyes of God is always a sin in any climate, country, or time. What is a traffic law in one city is not in another, but God's laws are not of such material. They are the same and just as operative in one place as another.

That is why there is just as much substance in the Sahara Desert as there is in the Bank of England — if you know it. Not if you try to demonstrate it, but if you *know* it. A little while ago I might have said there is just as much gold buried in Kentucky as there is in the Bank of England and been laughed at, but, "Behold, I make all things new." It is *all* enough — or do you want more?

And here comes that monotonous question again: "Do you believe it?" "Why, of course I believe, but why don't I see it?"

Do you understand a little? Are you peeping through the keyhole to the door of heaven and beginning to see that words are nothing when it comes to spiritual revelation? Do you believe that your Father is God? Are you a child of Love, or are you one of that grand army of unwanted people? You know what I mean, don't you? And you are beginning to see all about this illegitimate idea, too, and that it is not giving anybody license to handle with impunity the code of decency. But you see,

That Ye Might Have

don't you? And now you have this lovely word for just the right moment.

Coming across the country once, a young boy asked for a ride. The conversation drifted to home and parents. He suddenly turned sour and vindictive on the subject and finally, in a burst of emotion, said he was one of "those" creatures without legitimacy. I was as thrilled completely, for suddenly through me I heard the Voice speaking the whole truth to this Son of God. It thrilled me as much as it did him.

We rode on, and miles of country passed by unnoticed as he stepped right up into his place, freed from the whole belief. So many things were said to that one which cannot be put on paper, but the Voice will speak through you and give you such lovely illustrations and ideas, and the "glory of the Lord" will fill your whole house.

Presently we came to the place of parting, and when he left, he held out his hand and said, "I'll never say that again, and I'll never feel that again" — and was gone.

What I want to say to you is that *we* are the speakers of the *Word*. We represent no organization or person or book; we do not need to be known. We are the temples of the living God—and until you become this legitimate temple of the living God, you will be the illegitimate product of Adam.

And gradually you will place the seal upon your lips when someone tries to explain. You will be able to bring the something to that situation which will lift it out of its self-condemnation and fear. It must be terrible, the cold dark nights that people suffer from the idle gossip which "sinks ships."

"My grace is sufficient for thee." Do you hear? You don't have to have a formula. You don't have to give a talk or a treatment. You only have to open your mouth, and the Word will be supplied, the Word which will release as It corrects.

Doesn't seem possible, when you think of a huge battleship with all the men and engines, etc., that it could be sunk by a few careless words, to say nothing of the malicious words which are often issued intentionally. But it has happened, so watch ... .

It shouldn't be difficult when we actually begin to participate in the life of Jesus Christ. It isn't a withholding. It is a getting to the place in Consciousness where there is nothing to withhold.

You are a Son of the living God *now* because you have dropped off all the beliefs of a human father. There is a lot of rejoicing over you when the rightful heir returns to his place, about his Father's business. Selah!

Chapter IV

The Spreading Dawn

He is coming ...

He is coming whose place it is to rule. He is overturning and overturning until finally not one stone remains upon another, for the new thing has to be raised up.

I am not talking about the world; I am talking about you and your temple-body. I am talking about the Dawn of Revelation which is coming to *you* — the realization of your Permanent Identity. Like the dawn that slowly reaches out its slender white fingers, through the dark night of human thought, and draws all these misunderstandings and beliefs into the light of the full noonday, so this Light within you is gradually permeating your whole body and mind. You are being changed as the leaven changes the whole measure of meal until it is all leaven.

At a moment you think not, it happens. It has been going on so silently, even as a thief in the night, and yet it has been going on, undermining the superstructure of human thinking and its beliefs and bringing in place the realization of the "temple not made with hands, eternal in the heavens" — eternal in the Mind of God, who created it in His image and likeness.

Beloved, do you begin to see just what is going on within you? When you begin actually to appropriate the Jesus Christ Consciousness and are unafraid to take off at that new level, you will begin to experience this ever-increasing Dawn, this Spreading Dawn which is revealing a newness and wonder of life not recorded by man.

"Eyes have not seen, ears have not heard, neither has it entered into the heart of man the things that are prepared for them that love the Lord." You cannot see these things, for the light of the eye has been so obscured by the human thinking that you have been looking through the glass of your personality, which is filled with the Adam belief of race, color, creed, and even human family inheritance. And you cannot hear beyond the screeching of the human voice, which is offering life for sale. Yet Life is a gift from God!

As the termite, unseen, eats away the joists and rafters of an apparently solid house, which one day collapses, so the recognition of the Consciousness of Jesus Christ undermines the most difficult human situation. Sometimes it may seem that nothing is being done and that the old building stands there as adamant as ever. Day after day, the contemplation of the Presence and the recognition of your Permanent Identity is made, with no visible outward sign. But one day—ah! That one day, when the Spreading Dawn begins—"in the twinkling of an eye"—the thing which seemed so utterly beyond help or hope caves in, collapses, and goes down like a house of cards in a hurricane, and the place thereof is no more.

And *now* the degree of recognizing the thing as done and finished, before there are any appearances of it on the outside, is becoming more possible. We take off from the level of "it is consummated; it is finished" and actually begin to sense, know, that the signs follow; they do not precede. And so, in the face of the apparent no-change in condition, we stand, and eventually we see with the outer eye that which we find true with the inner.

Isn't it thrilling? Though you stumble and fall, you are not discouraged, and you will find within yourself a native ability to pick up more quickly each time you fall. For presently—yes, promptly—the Spreading Dawn comes. It radiates all around you. It covers the earth, your earth, your manifest kingdom, and reveals the wonders of it all. It reveals to you things which have been hidden for ages. They were always there, yet in the darkness of human thought, you could not see them. No wonder the command, "take no thought."

The human mind wants to fight this issue, for it seems so silly—and so it is. The wisdom of God as given by Jesus Christ was utter foolishness to the average listener. They even "laughed him to scorn" sometimes when He revealed more than they could grasp. How about you? And how about keeping it all secret until you can, in the Spreading Dawn, reveal it in all its glory? Don't try to *show* anything in the darkness of human thought, for even if *you* are able to sense it as true and real, the other one may not.

When this Spreading Dawn of recognition comes to any situation and clarifies it, you will never revert to that level of life again. There is no going back. It is wiped out forever. This lovely Light breaking through the density of material thinking neutralizes the supposed intensity and power of the relative law, disintegrating the human picture. Many times it will literally go to pieces, and always it will be passed out of the picture, for it is a shadow of human thinking and has nothing to support it in the Light of the presence of God. When the morning comes, when the Spreading Dawn appears, you loose the old belief and let it go because it is only a shadow. With the coming of Dawn—recognition—it no longer has power.

No evil thing can stand the light of day, and certainly the Dawn of recognition of the Presence in which you live, move, breathe, and have your being will take the power out of the ghost. Have you ever heard of a ghost story that took place at midday in the out-of-doors? You know why, don't you? You can see, and so you are not afraid. And it is just this extended vision, the coming of the Christ within you as the Father, that gives you the power over darkness, ignorance.

"Call upon me, and I will answer you." I did not say *perhaps* or *maybe*. But you can't call upon Me, your Divinity, until you know without question that *I* am God. Neither can you see or experience a ghost unless you are thoroughly sold on the idea there is such a thing, and then you can make it *appear*; but it cannot stand the Light, for it is a creation of human thinking and is sustained by it.

When once you come to the place of seeking the kingdom of God, not for things but because you have at last found that it is the only worthwhile thing in the whole universe, then you will find all of the promises being fulfilled without effort and without any atmosphere of the miraculous. It will be natural and normal and real to you.

Body and soul, at last being reunited after the long years of separation, makes the complete temple through which the Invisible is to be stepped-down into visibility. This body that you formerly found subjected to disease, fear, and lack; this body that was so dark with discord and unhappiness, suddenly by the union with its Soul becomes the temple of the living God, a place through which the Power can be stepped-down into visibility. Everything that is coming into your life will have to be embodied through you, or else it will be a symbolical thing without body—or a body without life. It is wonderful when you begin to accept this position of the resurrected body-temple.

And now through the revelation of the Jesus Christ Consciousness, the Dawn is beginning to spread through the darkened passages of your life. As this

The Spreading Dawn

light filters through, you begin to find that an actual searching of the joints and marrow is taking place. As you come into union with your Divinity, you experience the change in body and affairs in an almost startling fashion. Old disease and age-laden cells of your body are suddenly stirred to healthy life. And as the thieves and money-changers are driven from the temple, so the inheritance from a worldly father, the Adam dream, is cast out, for the human inheritance is mostly evil, based upon the idea of "when I would do good, I do evil" and "he is a liar, and the father of it."

Entering into this Fatherhood degree (the Father within) and actually living in the temple-body of God, you begin to understand how the so-called miraculous things which happened to Jesus can and must happen to you. It becomes natural and not a miracle. It is your *nature* that does the work and not just the name of a man back in history. You are conscious of the Presence in such a degree that the sick are instantly healed by the shedding of the Light from within you. "Who touched me" becomes a daily experience, for whether the human wants to heal another or not, when the Divine in you is touched, the "virtue" goes out, and the healing takes place.

When a person touches this state of consciousness and causes the Spreading Dawn of revelation suddenly to illumine the temple-body, it does not mean that this person is elevated to the consciousness of Jesus Christ in its entirety. Unless he accepts the consciousness and seeks the fulfillment of it within himself, he returns sooner or later to his former state. There were ten lepers healed, but only one returned to make the recognition (acknowledgment) of it as something other than a miracle. The others, no doubt, returned to their leper friends, who quickly disposed of the miracle as hypnotism; and again looking on the loathsome manifestation, the healed one more than likely returned to his former state, having experienced at best a momentary sense of freedom. The testimony and proof offered by his former associates would be sufficient to disabuse him of any understanding.

And so, "What is that to thee?" You give the Light—because you cannot hold back, not because you want to—whenever anything calls upon you, recognizing the Jesus Christ Consciousness within you to the extent that he believes. Then you "give" forth the healing. If he takes it, all well and good; if he does not take it, "all well and good too." When Jesus made not many mighty healings, it was not because His power failed. It was because His hearers could not accept it as real; for there is nothing in the human mind which can accept the God-dimension of Life. It is too good to be true; it is impossible—that is why it is possible to God.

"Shake the dust from off your feet." That is all. Jesus did not go about seeking to heal. He went about with this Light so that all might see and accept it, if they would. He was not trying to convert when He preached the kingdom—He was revealing. The more we preach the word of God, the more we drive people from the very thing we want to give them; but the more we show the fulfillment of it all and *let* them come into the Spreading Dawn of the New Day, the more we are approximating the teaching of Jesus Christ.

It is interesting that the very thing we *try* to do, we fail in doing, but the thing that is *let* to happen is the thing that quite naturally takes place. Jesus was the revelator of the heaven within, so wonderful and glorious and so far beyond anything man had ever conceived. So, Beloved, with you. You are a revelator.

"There is nothing hidden that shall not be uncovered" to the consciousness which understands the Jesus Christ blending, the body and soul oneness, the station between the seen and the unseen, the temple of the living God—you.

Sometimes in the midst of it all, your contemplation of Me will be so wonderful that you will literally experience the Spreading Dawn that is rushing on to the full noonday of expression, and in this lovely light of the Presence, you will see everything "that offendeth and maketh a lie" and every enemy and every hateful thing. What a thrill you will get when you see them for the first time and the old false faces tumble off and the true thing is revealed! What a lot of healing you will do in such moments when you meet Me in the Spreading Dawn!

Life will take on a new interest. Many troubled souls and people personally unknown to you will touch you, and many of them, in their despair, will be reaching up for something or somebody to help them. And even though you do not know them and may never contact them personally, you can and will, in this Spreading Dawn of revelation, give out such help as to make glad the heavy heart, and many times you will see the results, though they may know not from what temple the Light has shone.

This Spreading Dawn of which I speak is the coming of the Lord and Master of Life to His own vineyard. You remember in the parable how he [the lord of the vineyard] first sent the steward, whom the servants killed; then he tried sending the son and heir, and they killed him; and then he said, "I will go and destroy out of the vineyard all that maketh evil."

That is what is taking place with you. The coming of this Master to His own vineyard is the coming of your Father-Consciousness to His own embodiment, His temple, and He will kill the unfaithful servants and drive the rest from the vineyard. It is wonderful when you contemplate it all.

In the days of living in the mental plane, you were told you were a co-creator with God. That makes God a liar, because He said the creation was finished and done in six days and on the seventh He rested. Many people seem to think they know better and are still trying to create and work out inventions, most of which kill them in the end. Well, either you, with your co-creating ideas, are right, or God, who pronounced it finished and done, knows what He is talking about. You choose this day whom you will serve, whether you will enter now into the thing that is consummated and finished, awaiting your acceptance, or whether you will take centuries to learn by the painful method of attempting to create a universe which functions in evil and disease.

Recognizing this finished mystery and working from that basis brings the results of which Jesus spoke and proved and of which He said, "Go thou and do likewise." What man could do likewise from this co-creating plan? What man could produce five thousand loaves and fishes—or, for that matter, five?

This all seems vague and foolish to the human mind, and so it is. All the wisdom of God is foolishness in the eyes of man. And likewise, the wisdom of man is foolishness in the eyes of God, and unless you want to work from that basis, there is little hope of doing things which are entirely outside of that wisdom.

Remembering always that because *you* cannot make a thing happen with your best efforts does not say anything for or against the law governing such things. When you begin to see the way of Jesus, you will stop looking for some other channel for good to come to you but will first manifest it within yourself, and then you will not have to worry about the actual materialization. It will take place.

"Go into a city (a state of consciousness) and meet a man."

"But how will I know him?"

"He will have a water jug on his head."

On his head—have you ever stopped to think about the secret doctrine that is hidden away in the Bible? In the Orient, men never carry water; only women do it. Yet this man you are to meet has a jug of water on his head! Any danger of your missing it when you have the sign, the password?

Well, that is just the way the thing works. There is always something which gives you the key. Can you take it? Can you believe? And can you keep silent before Me? It's wonderful; more than that— it is all that the spiritual name implies, filled with light, filled with surprise, filled with hidden beauties and secret things of which you have never dreamed or imagined. But no matter how hard you *try* to demonstrate this wonderful Truth, nothing happens, for you are trying to *prove* it because you don't actually *believe* it. When you *believe*, you do a thing not to prove it, but it is proven because you do it. And so it goes.

If the thing you are trying to do through the time-space consciousness of human thought is actually done and you can quit your struggle and enter into the Jesus Christ Consciousness (the unity of Body and Soul), then you can do exactly as Jesus did when He lifted up His eyes to heaven and gave thanks for the finished, completed thing. The manner of its appearance was entirely out of His hands, as it will be out of yours; but you will know exactly what is to be done in order to make the unmanifest appear.

When the Light of this Jesus Christ Consciousness spreads over your universe, it searches out the hidden things of the human mind and thereby eradicates many unconscious defects from your universe. You will begin to feel the "weight" of personality falling away from you. Your mind will become dehypnotized from many things of which you are now unconscious.

Man can become so hypnotized by an idea that it becomes a part of him. I know a young American who took the name of a gentleman of standing and education who had passed on. He had known this man and consequently took on his mannerisms and made a perfect job of it; but the payoff came when he got his first job on the stage. Although he was handsome, manly, had a good, well-modulated voice—in fact, everything to make him ideal material for a leading man—yet he failed hopelessly in every part he attempted to essay. Eventually it was realized that in all his waking hours, he was constantly playing a character, and *that* character could not play another character.

Do you see that the character you are playing has not the ability to play another character, no more than if Ethel Barrymore should imagine she were actually Lady Macbeth and would try to get a job in another play to enact the character of Joan of Arc? Lady Macbeth is only a character and not real and could not possibly play anything else; but the moment Ethel Barrymore dropped the character which she had assumed and returned to her real self, she could then play any character she desired.

Do you get any light from this? When you drop this personality-character which you are playing and return to the basic character of your true self, there is a possibility of bringing out a new and different manifestation.

If you are hypnotized by some hereditary disease or other family failing, you cannot hope to superimpose upon this false character the idea of healing or getting well, for the character you are playing has no power of its own. It lives wholly by the thought-substance you are feeding it. So with poverty. People assume false characters of poverty and play them so well that they become hypnotized and then try by affirmations or words to superimpose upon this character of poverty the idea of wealth, but it is impossible.

You must return to your native self, the creation of God, made in the image and likeness of God, if you wish to bring out the new and lovely patterns of your Divine Destiny that are even now awaiting the call or the recognition. Upon the clean screen can be thrown the new picture; and more wonderful than all is the fact that when the Dawn of this lovely Christ-Consciousness comes to you, you find the screen of your life has not been changed by the hypnotic character studies you have thrown upon it.

Do you understand, then, the command, "Awake thou that sleepest, and Christ shall give thee light"?

The Spreading Dawn of realization will show you hidden things in your human thinking of which you did not know, and it will reveal in the storehouse of God the wonders that are to come forth through the temple of your body.

As we awaken from this hypnotism by coming into actual being of the Christ-Consciousness, we begin to see we are merely revelators of the finished mystery. We are here for the glory of God.

If you found yourself in a darkened art gallery and turned on the light, revealing priceless works of art, you wouldn't think of claiming that you had created them; you would merely say you had discovered them. And so when Jesus was confronted by the darkened consciousness of human lack and limitation, He "went unto his Father," and when that Light was turned on, He discovered the abundance of substance in the form and shape necessary to neutralize the pictures of evil. He did not create the bread as it apparently increased; neither did He add to the fish as He passed out five thousand of them. But all this is foolishness to the wisdom of man, and so again your attention is called to the law of secrecy that must govern anything you contemplate or perceive in the Mind of God.

Don't argue. "Agree with thine adversary quickly, whilst thou art in the way with him." If he believes that sickness is incurable, who are you to argue that you know better? He might ask you to prove it—and you could not, for remember, the God-power is not given in order that you may intrigue and amuse the curious.

And don't explain. No one will believe you anyway. He who knows needs no explanation—he wants inspiration. He wants the Spreading Dawn of revelation wherein he can live and be clean.

Just because you cannot do now the things which Jesus did does not mean that they cannot be done. Perhaps you cannot play a Brahms rhapsody at sight, but there are those who can.

"When the student is ready, the master will appear" is true and can be made manifest. When you are ready to *let* Me come into your consciousness and operate, *I* will do so, for *I* am your Permanent Identity, waiting for you to hear Me at the door so that *I* may come in and break bread (substance) with you.

It is wonderful, in this new dawning Light, to find that you are through with creating things or trying to help God. It is wonderful because then you find out what is the Father's business which you are supposed to do.

Beloved, it is so filled with the joy of expression that nothing which has gone before is worth a moment's consideration. Every man who hears My voice begins to live in a new fashion. It makes no difference where he is standing in the scale of things. He may be on the top of the stack; he may be on the bottom;

The Spreading Dawn

he may be sitting in the pigsty—it is all the same. The moment he hears My voice, he will automatically arise from poverty, filth, disease, chronic or acute beliefs in evil—and walk right down the highway of Life into the Father's house (consciousness) and hear the rejoicing and see the banquet table and feel the soft folds of the cloak.

It is all true, actually and literally. "Oh, taste and see that the Lord is good." Not the little good for the moment, but *good* in the great universal ways of life; good in a way you have never dreamed as possible; good in a measure that has no material counterpart. But to the jaded human palate, long since killed by the strong flavors of the world's cuisine, the taste is not noticeable.

Jesus knew that nothing but evil could come from human thinking, and He therefore "made himself as God"; and we are told, "as he is, so are we in this present world"—the very same thing, the identical substance and life. Do you begin to see that when you make your assumption as the child of God, you are taking only what belongs to you, and it is only in this assumption that the so-called miracles can be done?

All this lovely transition is done in the secret place, and you may return many, many times to the model, "the picture that is shown to you on the mount," but every time you return thereunto, you come away with a greater degree of its naturalness. It is natural and true and not some supernatural

That Ye Might Have

thing, when you once recognize the true nature of man. And when you understand, even in a degree, that your body—yes, this very funny old body, aged, diseased, filled with heavy scars of battle, filled with fears and limitations—is the actual, literal temple of the living God and is to be used for the purpose of showing forth the light of God, there is some reason for your existence.

In this realm of the Father-Consciousness wherein man contacts God, the universal Substance, man perceives the finished thing; he sees now how it is that the plowman shall overtake the harvester and that the plant is already in the field before rain or man to till the soil. And this very revelation enables him to cast the shadow into the manifest world, which man will call matter.

This book was done and completed before I put the first piece of paper into the machine, but I have had to return many times to "the picture shown to you on the mount" before I could cast the shadow into the relative world, and that shadow you are now holding in your hand as a book. Even as I write this on the paper, the shadow of the book you now hold does not yet exist in the outer realm, but it is complete and perfect in the realm of God.

Do you begin to see the truth back of all these parables and illustrations, none of which is adequate to give one millionth part of the wonder of it all? So in the Light of the Spreading Dawn, you will *see*— yea, you will *behold*!

In the Jesus Christ Consciousness, light shines forth and reveals the kingdom of heaven intact and perfect, and the glimpsing of this perfect, permanent idea is what brings the change in the physical realm. Can you imagine any physical change taking place literally, from a physical standpoint, which would have supplied eyes with perfect sight to a man born blind—that is without eyeballs or muscles to operate them?

Think about this a moment, and you will see that Jesus was not healing in the ordinary sense of the word, although it seemed so to the human sense. In reality, He was revealing that which already existed and that which was visible in the Light of the Christ-Consciousness; and when you awaken to this understanding, even in a degree, you will rest from your labors and lean on Me. The day of the hard taskmaster of *trying to understand Life* will be over in favor of the revelation of a law of a higher dimension than anything yet put into words. Do you begin to *see*, in the Spreading Dawn of this lovely revelation, what you do when you "heal" yourself or another and why it is stated that, "anything is possible to God"?

Imagine being asked, if you had been born blind, "Will you receive your sight?" Face a like question in your own life: "Will you be prospered?" What *could* you answer? Especially if you had been born blind and never had known what sight was, or if you had always been so deep in the picture of poverty that you never had known any ease or comfort? What would you say?

The human mind would say, "Yes," but the aside would be, "but I don't believe it possible"—and so it would *not* be possible. Why? Because you would be looking for ways and means of the incoming wealth or sight, and if you heard only from the human standpoint, you would be as much in the dark as ever about just how this utterly unknown thing could take place. The moment human reasoning comes into the picture, the inspiration goes out, for there is no reason to the Christ law. It is over and above all human law, science, and understanding. But there it stands: "Will you receive your sight?" If Jesus could not have revealed it to the blind man, do you suppose for one moment He would have asked that question? Then why do you suppose He asks *you* the same questions over and over again: "Will you be whole, prospered, happy, etc.?" What can you say? What can you do? *Hope* that it will come to pass?

The more you are still and contemplate God, the greater will be the manifestation in the physical world. The alignment of yourself with the spiritual laws of Life causes the distorted human laws to disappear. They are all put to flight.

When you see that you are a revelator, you will also understand that through the contemplation of this perfection, you are bringing into manifestation something which is original and different and which assures its success and power in the relative world.

A thousand composers could contemplate God and each one bring out distinctive music, original enough to make it instantly successful. So with you.

When you pray, you are actually contemplating the flower before the seed; and while all this seems foolish and worthless to the human thinking, it is exactly what you are told to do—to get the answer before the problem. And it is all so paradoxically stated that it throws dust in the eyes of the "wise" man.

I see where some learned professor has discovered that the Bible is true because it works out according to a certain chain of numbers; but can he with his numbers heal a sick man? Or raise the dead? Or even produce five thousand loaves of bread out of nothing? The only real interpreter of the Bible is the one who "goes and does likewise." Without works, it is all talk. Without works, it is nothing. But this need not discourage you; it should only cause you to dig deeper into the Consciousness of the Presence, to blend with It. If it is possible to a child, it is possible for you also.

Don't worry about your progress in Truth. "In my Father's house are many mansions," many stages and degrees of progress, and as fast as you absorb what is in one mansion you will go on to another. But during this period of absorption, there is much manifestation in whatever degree you may find yourself, and the moment you have absorbed it all, you will crack the shell of that degree and enter into

That Ye Might Have

another, just as the chick in the shell finally absorbs all the substance of the egg and breaks into another world of expression. This is a literal and practical thing, and it makes for a lovely sense of patience and revelation.

Going from glory to glory instead of experience to experience is the reward of recognizing the inspiration of Jesus Christ. It is wonderful, for the *I* always goes ahead and makes ready the new place of expression for you. "I go before you to prepare a place for you"—that is the Word. The place of expression you are entering is already prepared for you. You are going in to possess it, but you cannot possess it until you have absorbed everything in the former degree. Open wide the portals of your consciousness and receive and give forth thanksgiving for everything just as it is at this moment, for when this is done, the blessings will descend, and the appearances of bondage will fall away automatically; the shell will crack, and you will step out into your new day. From glory to glory—think on these things for a little while.

And so, in this Spreading Dawn of the New Day, if you are to "do the works that I do, and even greater," you must appropriate all the working equipment that goes with it. This is not acquired through the development of spiritual qualities or by long, hard study, but by the appropriation of your divinity, by the recognition of your permanent divinity as a reality.

The Spreading Dawn

The assumption of this is not nearly so difficult as it seems, once you actually believe in God and in the divine pattern, Jesus Christ. It comes over you gradually. You find yourself becoming conscious of new capacities that perhaps you cannot put into words, but you have a "feeling" that it is possible. You begin, in a way, to see "the man under the fig tree" and all that he has ever done and is doing; and with this sight you can understand and handle each situation, as it arises, not by the old method of preaching or lessons but by direct revelation. You can and will put your finger on the spot and relieve the tension.

Do you begin to understand a little? This Dawn is actually taking place, so don't get excited about the full noonday of expression. You are *in the Light*, and It is increasing in intensity all the while.

Slowly but surely, it is coming to you why Jesus "made himself as God." He knew there was no other way of manifesting the works of God. If you have to bring God down through the limited human thought, you have little hope of doing anything but a sort of touch and go manifestation, because you will always be fighting evil.

None of the works performed by Jesus were done by human methods or the consulting of human intellection. Over and over we hear, "My ways are not your ways," until finally we begin to *hear*, and the Light immediately begins to sift through. "Be of good cheer," —says the Voice, when you are tempted to turn again to the outside and see what has been done—"I have overcome the world." And then that pleading Voice goes on to invite you to "do the works that I do, and even greater." When this God-Consciousness arrives, all the half-gods of human belief and law flee before "the brightness of his coming."

Take all then; take the gift which is given unto you. Can you? Do you dare to assume the clear seeing to which Jesus so often referred? This gift of sight is one of the things which "eyes have not seen." It is one of the things which thousands may have caught in some way and turned into all sorts of channels of human fortune-telling and divining.

A thousand and one prophets proclaim the coming of the millennium and the New Day, yet it goes on from century to century, and we are in the midst of the most terrible holocaust ever recorded in history. The prophets are using every possible argument to prove that God is on their side, digging in the archives of dead papyrus and monuments and listening to old wives tales from the dark ages and proclaiming that God spoke through all these.

Well, they must have something to start the human ball rolling; but the message of Jesus was from the living God and not from some dusty material centuries old.

Do you begin to see that the power of the Jesus Christ Consciousness is indigenous to every man who will accept it? He doesn't have to be the seventh son of the seventh son—or daughter—nor must he have been born in the dark or light of the moon or under strange conditions or circumstances. He has to recognize that he is born of God, who knows all, sees all, hears all, and holds everything in His power. He then will be able to "read" whatever is necessary for him to read, without the aid of a card, a crystal, a talisman, or an ancient monument. Yea, without digging in the lore of the old prophets.

Yea, he will "leave all and follow me"—leave all the old ideas and follow his Permanent Identity back into the Father-Consciousness and will there perceive and know what is revealed to him in the Spreading Dawn of Life.

Chapter V

The God of Love

The air is full of preaching and beseeching these days—voices filled with fear, voices filled with condemnation, voices filled with prophecy, most of them telling of the wickedness of the world and mankind and of the avenging God who is waiting for His day to reap a rich reward of punishment.

What a lovely picture of God is being given to the world—a god as terrible as is possible to paint; a despot and an old tribal Jehovah apparently watching for only one thing—evil. Aha! He has laid a snare and lies about in the heavens watching for the poor helpless victim to get caught therein. And then—well, then the fun begins. And so the God of hate is presented to the world. Finally all the voices take on a more sanctimonious tone, and they invite you to worship this tyrant.

When Jesus came two thousand years ago, this same thing was in full swing. Priestcraft was busy getting followers by painting a God of fear. But He came preaching a God of Love, so lovely and so filled with understanding and mercy that people who heard wanted to worship and adore such a Being.

When they entered into this Love of God, for God Himself, then came down the showers of blessings from heaven—not because they had been good but

The God of Love

because they had merged into the Consciousness of God—and the manifestations took place, just the same as merging into the consciousness of the so-called God of fear brings forth the results of that state of things. Apparently it means deprivation of everything whatsoever that makes for happiness and brings on that "sharp eye" that is watching another to see if he is sinning, or if he is going to be punished.

When you begin to see the wonder of God and the loveliness of heaven, you will seek them not from fear but because their beauty is so impelling that you are drawn in automatically. The brightness of His coming is so great that all other lights are swallowed up. Actually, you are *translated,* or carried up in a cloud of light to the next dimension.

All this seems vague and nebulous to the person filled with the fear of God, and he glibly quotes: "The fear of God is the beginning of wisdom," not knowing that the fear here mentioned is the same awe you find within your heart when you see the display of some wonderful power on earth. You are awe-inspired at the performance of some wonderful opera or some great scene of nature.

Again the God of Love is coming into being, coming through the mass of false pictures of hate and revenge that are painted on the human mind. It is as if a character in a motion picture show should suddenly emerge from the screen in flesh and blood and prove to you that he was not the terrible tyrant he had been pictured on the screen. Presently, through the screen of fear and revenge, through the pictures of the tyrant God, emerges the lovely Presence that suddenly and actually translates you to the new dimension, wherein your lips automatically will breathe the prayer, "My Lord and my God." It isn't hard or difficult to understand the perpetual adoration of such a Being, and the praying without ceasing automatically goes on when you discover the God of love.

Yes, through the revelation of our Jesus Christ Consciousness, one day you will be sitting alone (maybe in a crowd) and suddenly He will come to you and will "translate you." And they shall know you no more after the fleshly mentality with which you have been identified before. It is wonderful.

You are in the Presence all the time, but you have been in the dark place of the fear-God just the same as your savage brother; you have been good because you have been afraid to be bad. But still you are in the Presence, and It keeps knocking at the door of your consciousness. And then one day you "hear my voice and open unto me." Yes, it is all literal and actual. You will experience this coming into your heart of the God of Love and the falling away of all the unlovely things you have taken unto yourself.

God becomes so lovely and glorious that there is no question about whether you should or should not worship Him. You cannot help it, for you are worshiping *Life*.

This Love-God in the midst of you will give forth such a Light that men will glorify God (not you), and you, being lifted up to this Light, or *translated*, as it were, will not again wonder where the daily bread comes from but will draw all things unto you. All things will be enough, and as you advance farther and farther into this translation, you will see how it is that the unseen Light of the Presence can and does, when recognized, penetrate the most dense substance of human thought, disintegrate it, and finally eliminate it. This Light enters into every situation and rids it automatically of the evilly-congested substances of human thought. There is no situation—past, present, or future—in your life into which this Light cannot penetrate.

Do you begin to see the protection that is given automatically to the "sheep among wolves"? A secret Light, more powerful than all the combined darkness of human evil, causes a secret undoing of whatever evil situation may be manifesting. No one can explain it, and the evil perpetrators of the picture begin to feel the "fear" of the Word, and the brightness of His coming will take care of the rest. You are the bearer of this Light that cannot be hid. Do you begin to understand?

"As many as believed were saved," saved from their own evil beliefs; and now they are saved through Love and not through fear, for that which is saved through Love is translated into *a new degree of consciousness* wherein is no darkness.

Remember, there is the secret undoing by the Light of God when It is cast upon any darkened condition in your life. Strange and wonderful are the ways of the Lord, past finding out. Yet gradually you are beginning to know something of this secret undoing of the power of Light.

Is it worth a little being still? Is it worth a little contemplation?

> Presently you will come to the "breathless adoration" of the Presence, so wonderful, terrible, and glorious. But see that you tell no man.

Chapter VI

Direct Action

A child prodigy without training reads a difficult piece of music that takes the ordinary person years to accomplish. A genius in mathematics glances at an apparently unsolvable problem and gives the answer without a moment's hesitation. It may take a trained mathematician hours to arrive at the same point. A professional reader of books turns the pages with such rapidity that it appears impossible to grasp more than one word on a page yet has the whole story perfectly in mind—characters, locale, and all.

All this is charged off to genius. The relative, slow-plodding, thought-taking mind disposes of a very troublesome manifestation with the bland words, "Born that way—genius, freak of nature, etc." If the relative mind stays too long on the subject, it sees this very manifestation has possibilities of undermining its most cherished plan of life, which is to work out your own salvation by the sweat of your brow. At the very outset, man is up against an ignorance so dense and black that it takes a whole lifetime even to make a pinprick in it with thought-taking methods.

If an ordinary musician stops practicing for a few years, he has completely lost his ability to perform anything worthwhile. He will say, "I am out of practice, etc." It is a losing game from the start. The demonstrator of health has nothing permanent; he must constantly "watch" his health. Apparently the only thing permanent in the conscious-thinking mind is evil. Everything worthwhile—health, happiness, wealth—has to be guarded from a pack of merciless laws. Life resolves itself into a grand free-for-all in which man is bound to be defeated. He has his choice of doctors, practitioners, medicine, treatments, pills, or affirmations, and all of them offer only temporary relief. Old age creeps on in spite of ten million affirmations about youth and a million pills, lotions, creams, serums, vitamins, and the like.

Not a nice picture—and yet a perfect drawing of what happened to Adam when he left the Edenic state and wandered into a universe of his own making, a universe made of the substance of his imagination, out of which have come all the grotesque ideas of life, built up and sustained by thought and verified by ten thousand proofs on every side.

It is not strange, then, that the Master said to people who apparently were awake, "Awake thou that sleepest, and Christ shall give thee light." "Awake and arise from the dead." That summons has fallen on deaf ears, which have taken it as symbolic of a momentary stirring of thought in an effort to bring something livable to the surface. Yet was this command a literal thing. It was and is a word which suddenly startles the man to action. It is something that makes the highest speed which man has attained as slow and laborious as a tortoise. When you *hear* this, you suddenly *feel* the uprising of yourself.

Many hearing this word will attempt to "put on" what they suppose to be spirituality. That is just about as effective as putting on the appearance of wealth or health. A few may be deceived by this false assumption, but the sad part about it all is that *you* are not fooled, even though you are semi-hypnotized into believing that you are getting somewhere. Presently the day of reckoning comes and you are "out." You rub your eyes and find that the "bridegroom" has already gone into the city and you have been asleep or without oil and could not see him.

In all the ways and means shown forth by the Master, Jesus Christ, we see nothing that savors of time or of coming of things into manifestation through thought-taking processes. It is all direct action—do, be, have, stretch forth, and a host of other wonderful releasements of the finished manifestation here and now, outside of and over all the slow ways and means of mankind and his best findings.

It makes no difference what testimony is set against the idea. "I have a way ye know not of" is sufficient to bring it to pass in your life in the face of the greatest opposition that all the conscious-thinking world can contrive. It utterly destroys every base of the human thinking and planning. It has nothing to do with brainpower, for the brain, as it now is, is the instrument of thought only. It is able to catch the far reaches of the inspiration of the Almighty, which causes all things to *be* instead of making them appear in accordance with the findings of thought. Dry land coming out of water; passing through fire without even the smell of it remaining; drinking any deadly thing; crossing the lake before you have time to get into a boat; moving through a crowd without touching anybody; increasing by breaking into pieces—every one of these movements completely sets aside the highest findings of the relative mind. It is wonderful!

"Not by might, not by power, but by my spirit." An element enters into the whole equation which has not yet been defined, catalogued, or pigeonholed by human thought, no matter how erudite.

Do you begin to sense something that is not being said or written but which is impressing itself on your consciousness, not upon your thought? For the moment you begin to analyze it or take thought about it, it disappears like the wind, which "bloweth where it listeth … and no man knoweth whence it cometh, and whither it goeth." So is it with the Spirit of man.

Do you begin to see this something of which it is written, "Eyes have not seen, ears have not heard, neither hath it entered into the heart of man, the things that are prepared for them that love the Law"? Do you begin to "feel" your way out a little into this new dimension? It is truly a "be still, and know (sense) that I am God" state of things. There is *no* other. All this miasma of evil that is about you, with its occasional demonstration of good, becomes as naught. There is no other. *There is no other*. It is wonderful!

"If I be lifted up, I will draw all men unto me." Once you conceive this Consciousness of which Jesus so often spoke, you will then stop the seeking and the getting and begin the natural appropriation and the normal assumption of *Life* that is not made up of the demonstrating of good over evil. That horseplay of the Adam life goes on generation after generation, and finally man is sick of the futility of it all. Civilization, as built up by man, comes to a crisis in high-powered war machines of death, armed to the teeth in order that peace may be maintained.

Prayer and the thing ordinarily called treatment are as far apart as the poles. The latter is a preconceived notion that if you please God with certain flattery, called praise, and make the right kind of combination of words, something will happen that ordinarily would not have happened; or a power will come along and put to flight the picture of evil. Well, sometimes it works, especially when the supplicant suddenly "touches" Consciousness; you need only to "touch the hem of the robe" to resolve instantly all the present pictures of evil into nothingness. This is not to say they will stay that way, for if you have not *the continuity of consciousness* to sustain such a picture, it will disintegrate and disappear about as strangely as it came.

Prayer, on the other hand, is the releasement through recognition of that which eternally *is*. It is like suddenly opening a floodgate. There is no need to coax the water to come through; it has been pressing against the gates for ages, just waiting the opportunity to pour forth. "Ye shall smite the rock," and make it gush forth the waters of Life.

What do you say? Going to "demonstrate" and get your hand fearfully bruised? Or are you going to smite the rock from the standpoint of consciousness and see the manifestation come forth both literally and symbolically. Do you believe, if you were actually in a desert and perishing, that you (I speak to you, the reader) could smite the rock? Would you dare try? Would you timidly make an experiment? Or would you, in the name of Jesus Christ, *smite* it?

Answer me!

Why will you fool yourself any longer with the asinine reasoning which results finally in the "yes, I know—*but*" state of affairs? Too long have you professed to accept the Christ and the Fatherhood degree of life and asked for a loaf, only to compromise for a half; and failing in this, have pleaded, "Well, just a slice for the momentary need." Then you have heard the ugly three-dimensional

Direct Action

mind say to you with the utmost disrespect, "Get under the table and eat with the dogs of the crumbs!" You don't like that, do you? But such is the result of trying to use this Christ-power on an old brain-foreshortened, thought-taking process.

Prayer is the manifestation of the kingdom of heaven here and *now*. It does not have to be kept in place by holding it in thought. There is nothing to disturb its even tenor. Prayer is like the massing of static electricity that suddenly, quick and terrible, bursts through and destroys false pictures. It is also as gentle and easy as the coming of dawn.

The direct action of God is as operative through your temple-body as it is through any teacher, lecturer, or leader. Jesus even suggested that you could and would exceed His works. To recognize the revelation of Jesus Christ in you is to cause this direct action to take place in your world and affairs and to precipitate manifestation, in spite of all the findings of the human mind and the relative ideas of life.

Touching this Power brings forth a full revelation on any given subject—causes the fool to become the genius, for genius is only the manifestation of being *en rapport* with the Presence. Everything that the human mind can possibly concoct in the way of a problem, even the so-called unsolvable ones, is perfectly known to this Consciousness—not through a process of thinking but by the direct action of the power of God. Everything that is ever done on the earth in the matter of manifestation is already completed and in operation in the Invisible.

Of course, the old human reasoning will attempt to think this out and will say that it is all foolishness; and for once, it is right, for everything that is true and lasting and of God is foolishness in the eyes of man. But remember that the reverse is also true. "The wisdom (wisdom, please note) of man is foolishness in the eyes (light) of God."

Do you begin to see why nothing is impossible to God? The human mind cannot reason beyond the confines of its own findings; it can go only so far, and it runs into the treadmill of the chicken and the egg, and the egg and the chicken. Which came first? Neither came first. The whole thing was, is, and always shall be in the Mind of God. The slow-thinking Adam-plane of life has to evolve from egg to chick, from seed to flower, unfolding and unfolding each step.

What a thunderclap when the Voice says, "Look again, the fields are white with harvest!" What must the human mind have thought of this *direct action*? All its best learning and wisdom thrown into the scrap heap of nothingness and foolishness. No wonder Jesus said so often, "I and my Father are one." He moved up into the "no-thought place," the Consciousness which "spake and it is (present tense) done." It is wonderful!

Don't let the old thought-taking process confuse you at the very moment when you are beginning to "be still, and *know* that *I* am God." When you are still in *this* thought-taking process, you will find out something you have been trying to know for ages.

"Only speak the word, and my servant shall be made alive." What a command—and a sudden and almost terrific manifestation! No one saw anything take place at that moment except the person receiving the healing, yet both the centurion and Jesus departed, dropped the subject, and went on their respective ways.

That is the pure, unadulterated, no-thought-taking acceptance that the Jesus Christ principle is not a speculative quantity but an actual releasement of the Finished Kingdom.

It is wonderful! "Speak the word." Would you dare to do such a thing? Notice that Jesus said, "I will come and heal him," no maybe or perhaps about it. This consciousness which was in Christ Jesus, and is potentially in you, does not have to wonder or guess or speculate whether it will be able to perform the releasement of the manifestation. It is able to "speak as one having authority," without knocking on wood or going through the silly superstitions of the human mind, trying to *make* it happen. It is a sure, uncompromising *Word*. It is successful every time, even when nothing happens on the other end, because had the person at the other end not been able to accept this Presence, nothing would have happened; but the "speaker" has nonetheless released the finished thing into being, and his part of the equation is done, completed, and finished.

To the human mind, this offers a possibility of running about "speaking the word" and then saying, "Well, I've done my work, and so I am through." This very statement would show how utterly one has failed in blending sufficiently with the Fatherhood degree to release the finished manifestation. "Be wise as serpents and harmless as doves." Say nothing, see nothing, do nothing; but be sure you see all, say all, and do all.

"My sheep hear my voice," and that is all that is necessary. Do *you* hear? "Behold, I make all things new." Do *you* hear? What would you give to have the old thought-filled brain made new? And what do you suppose would happen if it were? The *new* thing that takes place is an enlarged capacity, an actual change of the structure and substance of that part of your anatomy which is to receive and translate the new *Word* into increase and manifestation.

The genius plays the most difficult passages of a symphony with an ease impossible even to its composer, without effort, without taking thought, without struggle, and without enervating years of study. It is wonderful how a carpenter boy (Jesus) could do things that other boys could not possibly do and how He discovered that this Fatherhood degree of consciousness was resident in every man; though He also knew that man, until awakened, would go through the helpless infantile state, the

Sonship degree (be crucified) and would lie in his tomb until he self-resurrected. After crucifixion, the human has done all it can, for or against, and it is either, "Rise and walk" by the power of the recognized Fatherhood degree of consciousness, or lie there and remain dead. Who are you? And when will you begin the self-resurrection from your tomb? Answer me.

"Ask, and ye shall receive; knock, and it shall be opened unto you; seek, and ye shall find." What more could you want? Do you believe it? Or will you ask and then wait and wait and wait until you are flayed to death by thoughts of and about it all? Will you come unto Me and begin the direct action of the Word, or will you go to another or a book or a teacher?

The New Day has come unto you. You are merging into the Fatherhood Consciousness, above any further curse of the law and above any further field of experiences. The old thought-taking man has been filled with experiences; he has gone from one to another, swinging like a pendulum from good to evil, and at last he has dropped dead from its unrelenting wear and tear.

Now, as he assumes his Fatherhood degree, he is experiencing glory after glory instead of problem after problem. He is moving into reality from which there is no return into the shadows of the thought-taking process of the human mind.

And in this place of reality, he will be able to speak and ask and seek and knock—and find every one of these movements fulfilled instantly. He has the flower before the seed.

Chapter VII

Reincarnation and You

Ever since you tasted the forbidden fruit and decided that you, too, were a creator, you have been bringing forth the inventions of the human mind which, though sometimes beautiful for the moment, were always evil in the final analysis. All these false ideas of creation have been sustained by your belief, fed with the substance of human thinking.

You were created "in the image and likeness of God," a little lower than the angels, and given dominion over everything. And the book of creation was closed, and nothing is to be added or taken from it; and it was called good and very good. Yes, better than good—and that is the description of *you*.

All this is a far cry from the thing "born of woman," whose days are "few and full of trouble" and whose entire life is supported by human thinking and not by the Light of God. *Everything* that is born of the human thought is of few days and full of trouble and is a product of the human imagination. That is why Jesus, the Created One, could change any of the pictures of imagination, even death. And that is why you, when you arise to that place in consciousness, will see how it is that the so-called healing is not so miraculous after all, but natural and normal.

Under the belief in a power apart from God, man has come under a set of laws so hateful and so intricate that he sickens of it all. Everything he does brings its reaction immediately, or else a belief in karmic law causes him to re-enact the tragedies of his former life, an endless and hopeless chain of experiences that get him nowhere: He places himself under a fearful, inescapable destiny.

> Destiny waits on no man's will. Man made it, but can he change it? The sum total of his merit is arranged against the consequences of his sins, each at the end of the scale, and himself the fulcrum (*Black Light,* Talbot Mundy).

Jesus put it more simply when He said man has worked out "many inventions." Through a set of material laws founded on a divided power, man has worked out even a law of revenge which reacts upon him either as swiftly as a striking adder or as slowly as a glacier melting through centuries into one karmic situation after another. And in the human equation, according to the karmic law, there is no discount in the law of justice. So beautifully put by Jesus, "As a man soweth, so shall he reap."

There is no injustice, nowhere in all the universe, not for a moment. Justice—every atom of it including all the injustice! No one escapes his exact desserts or lacks his opportunity to learn.

Those on whom the seeming injustice is inflicted would do the same thing or something like it, its equivalent, if they had the power and the temptation.

They are learning the feel of the sting of injustice, learning not to inflict it. The unjust judge is reborn to a life in prison on a false charge. The usurer spends a life or two in debt. The cheat gets cheated. The cruel man suffers cruelty. Each to the fate his deeds have caused and each one to the destiny that he himself has earned. But what's the purpose of it?

It is true that the fool who tries to stop the wheels of destiny fulfills his destiny by being crushed under it (*Black Light*, Mundy).

But what's the purpose of it? Can you answer that one? What's the good of it all? Experience and problems leave most of us scratched and marred and with nothing better than a humble admission that, "It was good for our growth." Yet how could Spirit grow, since It is a changeless substance, without beginning or without end, complete and whole within Itself?

Gradually we are beginning to see that Jesus came for the purpose of showing man how to dehypnotize himself from the pictures of his various incarnations and to show him the "way back." He finds him groaning and wondering who will deliver him "from the body of this death ... to wit, the redemption of the body." And yet He plainly stated, "I can of mine own self do nothing," and He permitted Himself to function through the character of Jesus for the purpose of showing the whole gamut of human beliefs to be nothing but just that—beliefs.

When you took on your present character, unlike an actor you did not leave the old play and character behind but brought much of it along with you; and worst of all, you brought a balance sheet showing just what had to be paid on the old karmic debt, all the while adding to the endless karma of the next reincarnation.

What a stupid picture! Bound to the wheel of life that, moving upward, would throw you off into your real Self—if you could but accept the simple revelation of Jesus Christ. But instead of letting go, you hug the precious old beliefs and go down again to be crushed by the wheel as it makes its eternal rounds. You either survive the horrible experience of going under the wheel, or else it kills you and you take on a new character and begin again the "dance of life," a giddy affair governed by the laws "as for man, his days are few and full of trouble" and "earn your living by the sweat of your brow."

When Jesus came to the world to free it from this horrible curse and supply the grace of God, man was so hypnotized that he could not understand or accept the gift, and so Jesus was crucified—and would be again today because the mind is still so hypnotized with the reality of evil. That is why you are beginning to hear of the second coming of the Christ, in such things as, "Come apart from them," "Lean on Me," and a thousand and one other words which when *heard* will begin to free you from the endless chain of problems.

Jesus had to descend to the pattern of His Jesus incarnation in order to experience any evil whatsoever. That evil was all in His human destiny as Jesus, but anytime He wished to transcend, He "went unto his Father"—not a locality but a degree of consciousness—and the thing passed by with no expression. It was a cloud without rain. The child was stillborn.

Without having known or recognized His Permanent Identity, the one "made in the image and likeness," He never would have been able to set aside His human destiny. When the pictures of the false law were about to manifest, He immediately sidestepped them by entering into a new dimension and staying there. He was at "the other side of the lake," which was all outside of the human destiny plan for Him; and even on the way to the cross, He as good as said, "Well, if I didn't want to go through this to prove to you that even the karmic belief in death is nothing, I could call on My Father, the Permanent Identity, and twelve legions of angels would appear."

Are you beginning to see why the simple teachings of Jesus Christ are the only teachings which are worth considering? All the ancient teaching in the world will not reveal one-tenth of one percent of the power in one single *word* of Jesus Christ.

And the wonder of it all is that He said you could do everything He could do. Not only could you do it unto yourself but unto others. You could even raise the dead, which is "impossible." In fact,

He said you could offset every human law, and every "impossible" thing could be brushed out of the picture by you.

> Yes, Jesus came to show man how to transcend human destiny; but man mistook the whole lovely revelation for just another religion and fell down and worshipped a man instead of entering into the consciousness of the Presence and becoming *one* with it.

You are wondering why John Smith, who has been so good and true, never got to first base and why another, who had nothing at all coming to her, apparently skimmed the cream from the milk of Life without any effort; and now you are beginning to see the law: exactly what you have put into the universe, you have taken out. There is no escape until you come to the revelation of Jesus Christ.

This all sounds very dour, but in reality it is only what Jesus told us—and what we are only now beginning to *hear*. "My sheep hear my voice." It has taken us centuries, and we have waded through the muck and mire of hundreds of characters trying to find the way out of the maze of human inventions. It is only when you come to the consciousness of Jesus Christ that you begin to put an end to the human destiny and the human reincarnation. You begin to discover your divinity, which is only "a little lower than the angels," with dominion over everything on the earth, under the earth, and in the sea. Ridiculous when you think about dominion and then look about you! And yet there it stands, and only through the recognition of your Jesus Christ Consciousness can you return to your Father's house and find again the Garden of Eden, forsaken so long ago.

The hour is getting late. You are an avatar of the Word, and as you rise from the mire of human belief, you may yet have much of the mud sticking to you; but as you walk into the Consciousness of your true Self, you will find this mud dropping from you. And having arrived at the place of *Being*, you will speak from the plane of the Christ-Consciousness, dissolving the congested human beliefs.

"Come unto me and be ye saved." From what? Your human destiny and karmic beliefs. Lean on Me. The little John Smith, which has been standing alone for so many centuries, is finding what it means to give up and lean on Me.

There is much of human interest in reincarnation. You can easily trace many of yours out into apparent reality if you have the desire to do so. The human pattern is as fixed and real as is the divine, with this one exception: the divine, or fourth-dimensional, capacity of you transcends and utterly puts to flight any human destiny the moment you merge with your Divinity, no matter from what cause or how backed up by human testimony. It is therefore possible for a man with a so-called "short life line" to live to a ripe old age or a woman with all sorts of evil configurations in the heavens (as divined by thousands of people who have never looked

That Ye Might Have

through a telescope) to go on her merry way as an immortal creation of God.

Either you were made in the image and likeness of God or you were conceived in sin and born in iniquity—you decide that for yourself. If the former, then you are given authority over everything in, over, and under the earth and sea; and if the latter, then you must come under the curse (for it *is* a curse since it contains so much evil) of the laws of palmistry, stars, numbers, notes, colors, soles of the feet, and even locations. All of them are true in the degree in which they function. So is voodoo true and as workable on its plane as anything else—but remember: nothing that man says is wisdom, for it is foolishness in the eyes of God. "Choose ye this day whom you will serve."

When you begin to see this, you will stop the karmic sway of false human-thinking in your life, and the cat-and-mouse game will cease. You are created by God. Eventually you will "call no man your father," and if you call no man your father, you will have no human-father hereditary ideas to surmount. If God is your Father, you have no birthday and hence, no ensuing evil from having been born on a given day at a given moment in a given locality. *"The earth is the Lord's, and the fullness thereof."* Do you believe, or do you? You must answer for yourself.

Yes, I know that startling proof is offered; so was it when the wise men and magicians produced snakes which looked just like the snake which the prophet of God had produced, but—and there is the crux of it all—<u>the serpent of the man of God ate up the other serpents</u>. So does the power of God Almighty eat up all the quasi-powers claimed in ancient and modern teachings of evil.

Of course, this does not dispose of evil in the world at once, and it does not dispose of all the funny characteristics you see in yourself; but it does dispose of reliance on anything but God.

"But don't you believe the moon has any effect—remember the tides, the crops, and a hundred other proofs that can be shown?"

"I remember *one* thing—that I was created in the image and likeness, with dominion over everything on the earth, over the earth, on the sea, or in the sea."

And as I remember that, I begin to experience the *feel* that *God is in control of the universe,* not a star or a line or a color or a number. What say you?

From some hundred stenographic reports of prophecies of every sort and from every place, I find only a minimum of them took place—which is not discounting the gift of prophecy, but it is something to think about. The real gift of prophecy could no more be turned on and off, like water in your swimming pool, than could you (that funny little thing) turn God on and off because you made affirmations "at" Him.

Prophecy comes at the precise moment it is necessary. It is revelation and light that is given, but it is not to be used to find out every trifling incident in the universe of man's "wisdom." And so we begin to awaken from the dream of a power opposed to God and to see that all this reincarnation business goes on just so long as we think that we are born English, Negro, Jew, or Chinese instead of recognizing the fact that we are *born of God*, which recognition will cause us to fling off the garments of beliefs and superstition.

Do not misunderstand me. I do not discount the subject of astrology or palmistry or any other device to reveal the future. I know that "no man knoweth what a day may bring forth" is true—no man—except he to whom it is revealed for his own good purpose and reason. Do you see?

On the relative plane, all these pseudo sciences are true and real—but that is on the relative plane. For every time a so-called reality is set up, another comes along and changes the whole thing with a higher degree of human teaching.

Interpretation is so broad a field that it can lead many astray. "The letter killeth, and the spirit maketh alive." To see in a horoscope a man passing out may be true and false at the same time; he may be passing into a new state of things and dying to the old.

> "Ye can read the signs in the skies," but can you read the *signs of the times?*

When you ask for freedom from a karmic condition that is confronting you, are you willing and ready to take the consequences? Do you want to be free from a thing and have it too? I remember well a woman who said she was so tired of her home and wanted to get rid of it. Yet she broke out in tears when she returned home after a meditation and found it in ashes. The way of it all is not yours but God's. Be sure you want what you ask for, and be sure you are ready and willing to take the consequences of your prayers. These consequences are wonderful, but sometimes they may seem a little drastic on the surface.

A grandmother of sixty repeatedly said she wanted only one thing and that was youth. She wanted to be eighteen again. Suppose that prayer had been answered literally. Could she have taken it? She might have been turned out of her own house. Her twenty-year-old granddaughter certainly would have disclaimed her, and her sixty-five-year-old husband would have had her arrested as an impostor or a psychopathic case.

When you ask for something, you must see that it carries with it a set of new circumstances and conditions that will entirely change the present picture. Can you stand it? Could the grandmother stand being turned out of her own house by her own grandchild, who was now two years older than she? Think it over and see what this deeper revelation means; and then you will see why everything was "forsaken" when one followed and why this was a natural condition and not an imposed one.

Many people forsake the outside first and hope to make the inside come up to it, but that is getting the cart before the horse. When it is done within, the outside will follow naturally; but you must be prepared to step out of the karmic condition which is about you—to step out of the astral shells of belief that have held you for lo these many years—and enter into the New Day.

All this seems rather terrible, for it makes prayer a dangerous thing. I have written it to you from inspiration, knowing that you have the wisdom of God within you sufficient to interpret just what is being said.

Chapter VIII

The Day of Miracles

"Yes, I know, but the day of miracles has passed; Jesus was an especially endowed individual; there are incurable diseases and conditions in the world that nothing can help."

Yet the one uttering these very words would be shocked—yea, even offended—if you suggested that she did not believe in God. "Of course there is a God, or else how can you account for creation?"

So the human reasoning goes on, setting up the rather ridiculous picture of a God who has created a machine or brought out an invention which finally has taken the ascendency over Him, caught in a trap of His own creation! Looking out on a universe which He pronounced "good" and "very good," finished and done, He finds Himself faced with an infinite variety of problems over which He has no control. And so the human reasoning, which Jesus found "foolishness in the eyes of God," goes on its high-minded way, knowing something that God does not know.

What about it?

If you know of a single condition which cannot be entirely eliminated by God, then you don't believe in anything but a god of limitation. If you know of a disease which cannot be instantly dispelled by the

That Ye Might Have

Light of the Presence, then you know something that God does not know. If you know a single thing in all the intelligence of man which can defeat God, then you are still in the Stygian darkness of human thought.

Man has worked out "many inventions"—and what *inventions*. But possibly the silliest of them all is the system of ideas which professes to believe in God and yet finds Him as weak and anemic as a glass of water.

There is no use arguing about the set-up, for, to begin with, there are two levels of consciousness that are as far apart as Dives and Lazarus—there is no bridging the gulf. If you know evil as stronger than God, it is worse than useless to try to defeat it by praying to a weakling in the skies.

The Day of Miracles is past to the human mind. It always was past, for since the beginning of time, there was always a wisehead who could explain, by natural phenomena or illusion or something of the kind, how it was that every apparent miracle happened. Hence, the miracle of the birth of Jesus Christ was discounted and afterwards proven absolutely impossible. And so it is, to *that level* of consciousness.

The Day of Miracles is past also for the curious mind. It is too amusing to hear people say, "Well, if I could only see something done, I would believe." Might just as well sit down with an arithmetic and address it in the same manner. There is no reason

The Day of Miracles

why the curious one should believe. It makes no difference, and certainly there is no possibility of a curious, unbelieving mind ever seeing anything that the believing mind knows as a fact. The profane, ugly, human thing, which is so vile in its mentality that it would even tear the veil away from the place of birth to "see," is certainly turned awry and left to its speculations and findings.

"Well, I *tried* to believe." So did the child *try* to believe that two times two is five, but that did not alter anything.

God is not set up as the plaything of the vicious human mind that wants to peep and see and then try to figure it all out from his *scientific* basis of three-dimensional reasoning.

Yes, the Day of Miracles is past for the human mind. As we look out on the picture just now, we find the human thought has about run itself into a ditch. After thousands of years of "learning" and trying to make things better, it finds the entire world in flames and blood.

Happiness, peace, and contentment cannot be demonstrated by the human thought, for it depends on unhappiness, fear, and disease for contrast, in order to discern their opposites. It cannot hold to anything for long; the very atoms which fashion its manifestation are constantly disintegrating, dissolving. Age comes uninvited and unwanted; disease haunts every step from cradle to grave; poverty lurks in every cubbyhole of the human mind. And this mass of contradictions will stand and declare that there are conditions over which God has no control. From the level of a coal mine, quite a different concept of Light would be gained than from the level of the earth. There is nothing found by the human mind that is not subject to change without notice, and it is never the truth. It is at best a part truth; it may catch some glimmer of Light.

So there is no argument, and the man "whose breath is in his nostrils" cannot be convinced, because he insists on proof and no one can give proof, for God is not a jumping jack to please some silly child.

The Day of Miracles is here and now, when you arrive at the consciousness of the revelation of Jesus Christ.

"Oh, yes, when you arrive—but who has arrived? And how do you arrive?"

No one that you know and no one that you will ever know, for even though they stood beside you constantly working miracles, *your eyes*, looking through the conceit of your human wisdom, *could not see them*.

Even though Jesus Himself were to increase five loaves to five thousand and you were standing at His elbow, you could see nothing but a certain action going on, which you could easily explain, because what you see through your "glass darkly" causes

The Day of Miracles

everything to take on the order of the limitations of your consciousness.

God is not held a prisoner in His own creation any more than an artist is captive to his own picture. There is no pattern of life which can restrain Him, no picture of disease or human intellect which can withstand Him.

He plays upon the temples (bodies) of men when they are attuned to this new dimension, as a master musician plays upon the eighty-eight keys of a piano. The amateur human mind, which went its own way out of the Garden of Eden, has made plenty of discord as it fumbled over the keys. Its instrument (temple) has become full of thieves and unclean things and produces at best a broken melody of life.

When Jesus ascended to His Father within, the consciousness of His Permanent Identity, then the great forces of Creation were able to play through His temple, and the Day of Miracles came into being. Laws, conditions, and happenings which had no human foundation came into manifestation, and the former things of discord and lack were proven to be illusion.

The man with his breath in his nostrils still protests that a trick has been played on him, because it just couldn't happen! That is the only thing that does happen in God—the thing that just could not happen—and that is why He is God. If He could do only the possible, it would be as well to get a loudmouthed politician to do it, with plenty of publicity as an accompaniment.

So, Dear Heart, the next time you come to that idea that your condition or problem is a little beyond the God-power, just pause and remember that God is not caught in His own creation, and *you* are His creation; and suddenly you will begin to experience that "Day of Miracles" right *now*. It is wonderful.

Don't tell—show.

Chapter IX

White Elephants

First of all, *the size has nothing to do with it.* A half-carat diamond ring might be a "white elephant"—cause sleepless nights, fear, and even death. At the same time, a New York skyscraper might be only a good investment, with nothing but the usual business mechanics attached to it.

The white elephant is the thing, little or big, that you have asked for and brought into manifestation only to find it is walking all over you because it is occupying your entire attention. Any manifestation may become a white elephant. In fact, most people asking for "things" find they have white elephants on their hands. It is true that white elephants are the most expensive and the most sought after of all elephant-kind. Their price is beyond fine gold, but they are worth it only to those who know their value and how to handle them.

Sitting on the sidelines and watching the easy play of life in another, man imagines he would like to do just such a turn. But if he is suddenly precipitated into a like position, he goes to pieces and finds his white elephant, which only a moment before was so docile and well trained, trampling him to death.

There is a wide and terrible gap between wanting a thing and getting it. In that imaginary space, the

That Ye Might Have

action of the person about to receive the gift must be paced to a point where he can receive it, must be stepped-up to a consciousness of mastership over it. The changing of the daydream into reality is not as difficult as it is for the dreamer to become the actor and move with the new manifestation.

Strange as it may seem, almost every dreamer imagines he could do this easily; but he has not counted on a hundred and one things that take place the moment the change to *actor* comes to pass. Being able to take your good is more difficult than it appears, and yet it is easy when the consciousness is equal to the thing asked for. "Be careful what you set your heart on, for that will come to pass" is good, sound advice.

A man eternally seeking riches once precipitated, through a lottery ticket, half a million dollars and dropped dead when he received it. Thousands of like illustrations might be given. A reformer imagines that he can carry out his Utopian scheme easily because he is working with robots that obey his every wish. Let him come suddenly into the desired position at the head of an army of men and women, each with a mind of his own, and he finds the situation fast slipping out of his control. He had not counted on all this.

It is easy enough to say, "Let the child be born," but just let this take place and see what happens in the universe in which the speaker lives. Everything has been temporarily affected by this advent. It is as if the atoms had all been disturbed and were whirling about furiously, trying to get settled again. If the speaker can "stand" past this point of confusion, he will be able to care for the child. If not, he will go to pieces and lose everything. All this difficulty comes from allowing the *personal* to come *again* into authority.

One of the great laws back of being able to tame the white elephant is the knowledge that nothing is of any importance. Manifestation is held together only by consciousness and is a vehicle of expression which must give way to progress. An engine has no power of itself. An egg must crack up and disappear as egg if it is to accomplish anything, or else the next stage of development will not take place, and so with the seed.

The very unimportance of it takes away the fear of it. Nothing you are going to do is of any importance except it be a means of expressing God in the universe more clearly; and inversely, everything is tremendously important. If you make anything unusual or unnatural of the new manifestation, the vehicle will dominate the expression and will so inhibit it that what finally appears will be practically worthless. Hence, an inspired person, if he considers for a moment the importance of what he is doing, will descend to the level of stage fright and get his body in the way to such an extent that his message is completely choked by personality.

If you can magnify the Power within you and go forth with the highest sense of integrity, which is the divine carelessness of which it is advised, "Be careful over nothing," you will keep pace with the new step and find the white elephant docile and easy to manage. It is wonderful when you can "go" and really abandon yourself to the "going."

Divine carelessness, far removed from the human sense of carelessness, is that sign of power which is going "from glory to glory." As fast as the shell of the manifestation has served its purpose, it is cast aside, and a willingness, yea, even gladness, to see it go takes the floor. You are moving with the Power, and there is no limit to where you can go, even unto overcoming "the last enemy."

If the voltage of electricity is to be increased, so must the wires and receiving instrument be enlarged. As you go "from glory to glory," so must the consciousness be deepened or expanded to meet the new level of manifest power, or else havoc results. The deepening of consciousness comes through a steady contemplation of God — here, there, everywhere, in every situation, in every person, place, and thing. "Heaven and earth are full of thee" — contemplation on the omnipotent, omnipresent, omniscient God, who lives, moves, breathes, and has His being in you and in all manifest things; a deep laving in the thing called *life impersonal*; an exploring, as it were, of the reaches of Infinity without so much as a thought of *you*, the personal manifestation. All this will deepen your consciousness of that Power upon which you are calling and will give you the right to call, the right that always comes of knowing the basis of your reliance.

Too long we have depended on what we have been told or what we have read and have been busy trying to make "It" work. Eventually we find that "It" does not do our bidding. No father is going to be completely driven into submission by a child. Stop thinking of power in terms of your little personal God and conceive this *Presence* just once, and you will find new and lovely capacities opening to you.

Glory in the Presence! You are supreme over everything you have ever desired or thought. You are supreme in your own heaven and earth, and you are master of it all when once you realize this All-Presence and let the rest of it be under the government of this Principle instead of under you. In this very simple way of life, you will not then be affrighted at the manifestation for which you are calling.

It is well to ask yourself whether you could accept the "demonstration" which you are trying to make. What would you do if you suddenly precipitated your dream of immense wealth? Remember, you have been used to handling only a small amount of money. You would have houses, lands, cars, servants, riches, and all leaning upon you. Of course, the human mind easily says, "I could manage it nicely," but unless the consciousness has been deepened to a point equal to sustaining and handling such a situation, you would go to pieces and blame everything else for the failure.

Further, do you actually believe that what you are asking, you can or will receive? Do you believe it is possible for this to come through the no-time-space process of which Jesus speaks? You see what a lot of housecleaning has to take place before you are ready for the things for which you are asking. Once you have perceived it possible and once you have accepted it as a finished thing, it is then ready to come forth.

It would have been quite easy for a human Jesus to have been trampled to death by the white elephants of manifestation. Think of the importance of feeding five thousand from virtually nothing. That might have floored Him. The fear of it all might have overcome Him; greed might have come into play. A thousand and one things might have happened had He descended to the level of things as they seemed to be. It is wonderful to pause and see just what is going on in your own life.

A lady once complained to me very bitterly that although she was ready to "speak the truth," she had little opportunity and that when she did have a chance, she had too small an audience. This she told me in the anteroom of a lecture hall, crowded to the doors. Feeling sure that she was sincere and was ready to go forth the moment an opportunity offered, I went to the intervening door, opened it, and said to her, "Here's your manifestation. I shall go in and announce that you are to lecture."

The woman blanched and gasped, "Close that door. Close that door!" She sank to a chair and began making all kinds of excuses, denying the fact that she had ever asked to lecture to large crowds. She ended her tirade by saying, "You have no right to interfere in my life. I have always managed through the love of God to make my own demonstrations." The white elephant had trampled her to death because suddenly it had become important. "All right," I said, "You don't have to lecture." Suddenly the huge bulk of her white elephant dropped before her, and she mounted his carcass triumphantly.

So until your consciousness is deepened to the place of accepting your good and being able to treat all manifestation and expression as being relatively unimportant, you will be floored constantly by that which you are seeking.

No matter what it is you want, no matter what it is you are going to do, it is all unimportant if your consciousness is equal to it. The next time you go bagging game, don't be affrighted by the white elephant you have been hunting in the jungles of human thinking; for he will be docile and gentle and will kneel for you to mount, if you realize the unimportance of it all.

When these books suggested themselves to me, I was naturally delighted with the idea and proceeded to insert a piece of paper into the machine. Presently it will be in your hands. But if I stop to think what launching them entails, I see a thousand and one things entering in to dismay me—the hundreds of hours of work, the correcting, proofing, publishing, and distribution; it looks like a whole flock of white elephants. Yet as I go from letter to letter, presently it will fall out in perfect shape, everything coming to pass at the right moment.

Chapter X

The Inspiration

When the inspiration of the Almighty has come unto you, he shall lead you into all things, show you all things.

Until one perceives that the "John Smith" consciousness is concerned with things and "taking thought," one can never experience the new dimension more than in temporary flashes. It is true that from time to time the unenlightened mind catches glimpses of this changeless Christ-mind, and in so doing, for the moment brings to pass something that would not otherwise have happened. If one is unfortunate enough to have experienced one of these rare miracles, he will more than likely spend the rest of his life trying to make it happen again or living on the dead husks of memory, sifting through his mind all the incidents of the event and adding to them from time to time.

Jesus knew that nothing whatsoever could come to pass by taking thought. He counseled against it and called attention to the fact that "no man by taking thought could add one cubit to his stature." Yet until man has passed through a long, ugly course of trying to make things happen by thinking about them, he is rarely ever ready to stop taking thought.

It seems almost impossible to explain how we arrive at the "no-thought process" of life, which is

That Ye Might Have

pure Recognition. The moment man becomes conscious of *the Presence* as the only actuality, he is no more concerned about the out-picturing of that Power, knowing that he has absolutely nothing to do with the how, why, when, and where of manifestation. It comes by a way that no man knows, and only the ignorant will attempt to fashion a mold or a way for the substance to come forth. "I have a way you know not of."

No sooner does man perceive by pure recognition of the Presence this changeless consciousness of God Almighty than he utters a statement of the fact, "It is done." This may be in many forms, and he may exclaim, "All that the Father hath is mine," and proceed to appropriate this gift. The ignorant bystander, having heard these words and seen the results, naturally thinks backward and concludes that the manifestation came because of the affirmation; whereas the affirmation was a mere statement of that which was recognized as a reality. Back of every affirmation is the actual substance which causes it to be uttered, or else there is the mistaken human mind which thinks to move the Invisible by the utterance of words.

Words are nothing. Even sounds are nothing, since a word-sound in one language may mean something entirely different in another one; and certainly the grouping of letters and words, being different in every language, gives us a picture of the hopelessness of words as a means of changing the

The Inspiration

unchangeable. The *consciousness* of the Word, however, is the same in any language, and that is why Jesus Christ could have healed a man even when speaking a language entirely foreign to him. The word-sounds He uttered, when He had finally made His full and absolute recognition of the Father, signified nothing except as an explanation of that which had taken place and was about to appear.

Every so-called miracle recorded in the Bible took place before human thought could have time to fashion its ideas. "In the twinkling of an eye" does the unseen become seen when it is recognized. Then flows the affirmation and the confirmation, or the thing "made flesh."

Jesus is constantly admonishing His followers not to consort with the man they pass on the highway and the man "whose breath is in his nostrils," because such a man is full of thoughts and words, and the one who is in the business of "taking thought" is in the business of dissecting the body to find out where the vital spark is. He never finds it because his ignorant seeking has killed that which he sought.

"Be still, and know that I am God" gives no room for speculative thought. Be still, and *know*. When you are *still* and know that two times two are four, there is no speculative thought, wondering whether it will work or how it will work or when it will work. Be still.

"When ye pray, believe that ye receive," and it shall be so. This *believe* is used in the sense that it indicates something beyond thought, for no thinking human would believe that he had received a thing that he actually had not, and his "thought," therefore, about the whole matter would be in the nature of self-hypnosis or at best pure imagination, either of which would produce nothing better than "clouds without rain."

His *believing*, however, as used in this instruction, would be an ascending straight into the creative plane of life and therein appropriating and accepting the substance of pure Spirit, permitting It to solidify and form into Its own perfect patterns. His *belief* would be stayed on the actual substance back of everything rather than on its embodiment. This vital substance would then take on its own manifestation, "by the way ye know not of." His prayer, therefore, would be answered, because it was answered before he asked. "Before ye ask, I will answer, and while you are yet speaking, I shall give it unto you."

> You see that the recognition of this "finished" mystery, the pure acceptance of this vital substance of life, would be there the moment the spiritual lack was experienced, and while he was making his affirmation of what he had perceived, it would be given to him. "While ye are yet speaking, I shall give it unto you."

It is wonderful, the simplicity of the Christ-teaching. The "consider the lilies" means something when you consider just what it is and understand that no amount of toiling or working or gathering of

The Inspiration

symbols into barns is going to give anything but a temporary relief at most. And perhaps not that.

From the thought-taking point of view, it is worse than useless to say that there is no sin, sickness, or disease, for there is a superabundance of all of these on the thought-taking plane. In fact, they are all the products of thought, as is every other evil that is known to man. "Nothing is good or bad, but thinking makes it so" and "as a man thinketh in his heart, so is he" indicate that all the evil and trouble in the world emanate from thought and are sustained by it.

It is likewise impossible for one resting in this thought-taking plane to do anything more than Jesus did. You will note that Jesus "went unto his Father" or "raised his eyes to heaven," and then He stopped taking thought and perceived the pure Presence within everything, instantly available to the one recognizing that truth. How, why, when, or where does not enter in. All this manifesting is entirely outside of the possibility of thought-taking since it is going to reverse every bit of thought and release a flow of manifestation that will assuage the temporary lack at that very moment.

> Unless the consciousness is stayed on Me, the flow ceases the moment the lack is filled, and, usually, man returns again to his hunger. ✓

No matter what a man is seeking or desiring, its basis is a spiritual lack. His urge may be so far removed from what he deems spiritual that he may see it as something almost evil in the eyes of the rest of the world. When a man is hungry or starving, he actually wants that hunger appeased and cares nothing about the food itself. He wants the void filled with something that is as near substance as he can imagine, but in reality what he is seeking is the substance of Life which is God.

> When a man becomes conscious of this truth he will never hunger or thirst again, for he will have drunk deep of the inspiration and tasted of the real substance.

Then it may be manifested in numerous material ways at any place and in any manner, and certainly it will be manifested entirely outside of the so-called laws of man, if that is necessary. If it is not necessary to bring it through by what the world calls a miracle, it will come in a humanly natural, though perhaps unthought of, manner. We see Jesus at one time feeding five thousand, breaking five loaves into increase; at another time we hear Him asking, "Children, have ye any meat?"

You begin to understand that to sense this new dimension is not to make a miracle worker of yourself. It is anything but that; it is merely that the harmony of heaven here and now may be sustained through the chaos of human thought. It is all wonderful! You will "go forth in weeping, but ye shall return in joy," for the secret that is to be made known to you is that you are "in the Spirit" and no more under "the curse of the law." You will become so

The Inspiration

conscious of this Presence and dwell so constantly on the creative plane that miracle will follow miracle. But they will not be miracles to you; they will all be the natural expression of Life filling the spiritual lack that has been felt.

We have long since realized that words often indicate the actual absence of the subject under discussion. You never hear a millionaire saying, "Money, money, money, substance," and yet you have heard whole roomfuls of people shouting this untruth as an affirmation. You knew it was untrue because if they had money or substance they would not be shouting for it. A man who is breathing normally does not shout for breath, nor does a healthy man constantly affirm his health.

As fast as an idea is appropriated, its substance is consumed, and the skeleton is thrown away. "Eat my body, drink my blood," throw away the skeleton. As soon as you eat the egg, you throw the shell away. And now that we have eaten up the substance of the mental egg, which had for its glorious motto "mind over matter," all that it had to offer has been incorporated into life, and we are again in the desert. The new idea, as old as time itself yet new to the individual, has come. *It is the pure recognition of the real teaching of Jesus Christ—unadulterated, unchanged, and literal.*

The fact that very little healing is being done among us today through the thought-taking process is proof enough that we are finished with the mental thing. We have arrived at a point of saturation, and if we do not move on, we die in the shell, just as the bird which does not peck its way out of the shell will die, though it has all the potentialities of a free and glorious life.

You are literally entering on the plane of creative Spirit because the self-glorification is gone, and you are come to the place of "doing the works" literally.

> Believest thou this? Then you will be silent and serene and not aloof and stiff-necked or loose-mouthed and blatant. You will "go your way," you will *know*, and nothing else matters.

Chapter XI

Experience—and Straightway the Spirit

And straightway the spirit descended into the waters and troubled the waters.

And then the healing took place. The calm surface of things was suddenly thrown into apparent confusion before the new pattern or idea could be made manifest. So it is with every change that must happen to man. The moment the spirit of the Presence enters into the proposition, the waters of life at that instant are troubled and shaken and stirred up, and the whole nature of them is changed.

Misunderstanding this movement of the Word, man often thinks nothing but chaos and disillusionment have resulted from his best prayers and supplications. If he judges from the appearances, at that moment he is sure to draw an erroneous conclusion and run away from his own good. So that the new order of things may come into being, it is necessary for the old order to change, be broken up, and pass away.

In order that an egg may cease being an egg and take on the new manifestation, the whole outer wall of its universe must give way and appear to all intents and purposes as complete chaos and destruction, but in reality it is freedom for the new manifestation.

The poor little helpless manifestation that finally comes through the chaos looks about in a world of strange newness and fearful things; but presently he moves out of the confusion and begins claiming and assuming his rightful place in the new scheme of things.

> The next time you have "prayed" and the manifestation precipitates you into the confusion of change, recede into the inner sanctuary and there abide until the dust storm of human thought passes by.

When you do this, you will see the glory of the Lord revealed and the fulfillment of your desire, here and now.

> And then presently there is the telescoping of the time-space idea, as we move more and more into Consciousness and away from the thought-taking process.

Presently we shall be over at "the other side of the lake" so quickly that we have not had time to go through the confusion of the change, and we shall see the manifestation of the loaves and fishes without the excitement of the human thought because we have entered deeper and deeper into the consciousness of the Fatherhood degree, and all time and space have become null and void.

As we stand in this holy state of contemplation, even *now* the Father has gone out in all directions and has gathered all the thorns and evils out of the son's life and cast them into the flames of hell. It is wonderful! Even now this great neutralizing power has gone out into manifestation, even as you read. The results will be magnificent and amazing. Suddenly all the evil and its progenitors will flee and disappear into the wilderness of human thought.

Speak the Word! Speak the Word! Speak the Word!

Let us suddenly sweep all this old past tense evil out of the picture and be done with it. So white-hot is the consuming fire that the place thereof shall be no more, and even the memory of it shall pass.

Do you see what is taking place at this instant in your life? Nothing that has gone before is of any importance. Such a complete sense of wiping out has taken place that it cannot be remembered any more. When it is out of your consciousness, it is out of all minds. It just cannot be remembered any more. It is wonderful how the consciousness of the Presence has come unto you *now*.

Nearly any businessman will tell you that upon the taking over of a new business it is first accompanied by what appears to be failure. For some time it seems that everything is going in the wrong direction and nothing in the right. A thousand and one things present themselves for adjustment, which only add to the conclusion that his prayers have brought ruination upon his head.

It is at this precise moment that he needs most of all to "be still, and know that I am God" and that "the Lord in the midst of thee is strong and mighty." Not with the idea of overcoming evil but with the idea of seeing the new form of power hold forth and show forth.

> Nothing can possibly happen that the love of God has not permitted when you work this way, and you stand in the dust storm of your own making until suddenly it is cleared away by the breath of God, and you see the salvation of the *law*.

When health comes to your temple, it means the throwing out of all sorts of evil things and conditions, and many times you experience a worse state than before you prayed, just before the new manifestation comes into being. So *be still*. Be sure that you want what you are asking for, because it is fraught with the confusion of change in order that the changeless sense of life may be fulfilled.

> In the new day into which we are moving, the time for the complete swallowing up of conscious thinking is at hand; it is this slow process of arriving at a given end that causes all the trouble. Jesus knew that conscious thinking would only bring confusion, so He stepped-up His consciousness to the Fatherhood degree wherein "it is done" was the order, an order not brought about by a long and logical series of conscious-thinking steps.

We may mentally say or declare or affirm, "Arise and walk," and the patient tries over and over again, but it is not until he actually *does* rise and walk that he understands the difference between the thought-taking process and the Consciousness which reveals. At that moment of revelation, every bit of human fate and every speck of human logic and law dissolves instantly into nothingness, no matter what confusion it causes in the mortal mind world. No matter if it throws a monkey wrench into the greatest piece of machinery of human thought ever conceived—it is all nothing.

Everything that stands in the way of this Consciousness is thrown into convulsions of its own confusion and is in the way of complete and absolute annihilation. "Stand fast therefore with the liberty wherewith God has made you free, and go not back again to your former bondage." And when you have come to this place, you will find definitely that "the former things have passed away" and "shall not be remembered nor come into mind any more."

> This sudden release of the Consciousness which transcends all human thinking is so terrific to the towering wall of human thought that it shatters even the last vestige of the thought-taking pictures of evil and chaos. It has been known to go back four days and destroy all the thought-pictures of death and bring to life again a man whose body was in a state of putrefaction and decay (Lazarus).

Think it over and hear the roaring old human mind say, "It can't be done." And it *can't* be done by thought. But it *is* done by Consciousness; so you can enter into past conditions and release your good and destroy all the evil manifested there. It is wonderful! Even at this moment, the leaven is at work and is going into the tomb of yesterday and releasing your life and manifestations from the dishonesty and beliefs of yesterday.

You have never lost anything, never had anything taken from you, never had a law operate against you illegally, never met an unfair situation that at this moment this Consciousness is not setting right. And in the setting right of all this, those who were in power and held such evil sway over the situation must and will answer for their part in the fiasco from which you have suffered.

Do you hear? Do you begin to see that we are the sons of God merging into the Fatherhood degree and that we have a right to the kingdom of heaven here and now and a right to offset all the times that evil has seemed to triumph over God? "Who is so great a God as our God?" And even at this instant, as we glory in the releasement of this Consciousness, the results will take care of themselves. Evil which came at you in one way will flee in ten, delighted to escape destruction.

Whither can evil go from this power? Heaven and earth are full of the Lord, and this power is operative the moment you stop the thought process, assume your Fatherhood degree, and manifest the Consciousness—a Beethoven, hearing his entire symphony as a single note; a Son of God seeing the finished mystery instead of all the tiresome thought patterns which are called experiences.

Injustice? No such thing is possible in the Presence. All the injustice in the past is suddenly righted, and the blessing of the Lord descends on you like a cooling rain and like a rain of fire on him who set up the patterns of injustice. It makes no difference how long ago it happened and how completely your enemies triumphed against you.

> Your enemies will flee,
> and their reward is with them.
> So rest secure in this
> sensing of the Presence.

Chapter XII

Let No Man Deceive You

Little children, let no man deceive you ...
Many will come in my name ...

The watchword and the warning fires have been set. If you follow no man, you cannot possibly be deceived by any man.

If you follow Me, you cannot be involved in any personal teachings, organizations, opinions, and beliefs. There are no by-laws in the kingdom of heaven, and there are no lessons and classrooms. All these are man-made. The law of God is revelation. It is not a constant stream of ugly experiences and problems. Life is not something to be "worked out" but something to be lived; but as long as you live with the *name* of Jesus Christ, instead of the *nature*, you will experience the emptiness of life and go through an endless stream of evil pictures, all caused and sustained by the conscious thinking.

To understand the name of Jesus Christ as the *nature* is to produce certain and definite results to your prayers. For in the nature, you are one with the Principle of it all and are automatically expressing what the Principle has to say or do through you. *"I will walk in you; I will talk in you, etc., etc."* —but it might be added, *"You cannot make Me do either of* these things by simply calling on the name *Jesus.*" Many have said, "Lord, Lord," and there is no Lord, in spite of the promise that "if you ask, you shall receive" and "if you call, *I* will answer you."

"With all thy getting, get understanding." So in making the differentiation in the *nature* and *name* of Jesus Christ, you enter into a stage of self-revelation or begin to experience some of the things which eyes have not seen, nor ears heard. In other words, you find the impossible and the unexpected fulfilled with ease and precision.

When once awakened to the revelation of Jesus Christ, you will never again wonder about the rightness of any revelation, for you have a foolproof measure for it all. Everything has been stated so simply by the Master, and now that you have entered into the nature of it all, you will find the interpretation and will know whether it—what you are hearing or seeing—is of God.

"Many shall come in my name." It is most amazing that hundreds of people who believe they are teaching the truth are going against every known concept of Jesus Christ. They come with all sorts of secrets and mysteries (none of which belongs to the teaching of Jesus Christ) which are "given by vision," (so they say)—many secret formulae, private revelations, and teachings. Some of them go so far as to admit that they are the only ones who have this revelation or the only one to whom it will be given. And stranger still, many people believe it and thereafter are unconsciously worshiping a teacher or leader. Presently they are led down a path which ends in complete disillusionment.

In today's jargon, mysticism is a much abused word. Everyone claims to be a mystic, from the lowest fortune teller to the most exalted swami. The true mystic is not known of man by his eccentricity—and being a mystic is not a trade but a necessity as one advances straight into the Consciousness from which he came. You can no more help being a mystic than you can help growing up as time passes, if you are on the true path.

This being a mystic does not set you apart as a curiosity who advertises strange and wonderful experiences for the purpose of selling a course in mysticism. You cannot buy or learn mysticism from another; you must discover it within yourself. When you have found this *pearl of great price*, it will be too precious to peddle it in the streets of life. It is ridiculous to exploit God like a glamour girl of the movies.

Do you begin to see that the doctrine is "not mine, but his that sent me" into expression? That the revelation is from *no man*—it may be *through* him, but it is never *of* him.

"Little children, let no man deceive you." Do not follow any man—follow Me. Do you begin to see and understand what is the height and breadth and depth of God?

"Prove me and see." Do you know any ancient or modern teacher who can say as much? Do you know of any fantastic law that cannot be stated in simple direct words by Jesus Christ? I have listened to much, read more; and after volumes of teaching, the twenty-fifth lesson is one of sheer simplicity and simple self-revelation as stated by Jesus Christ.

Yet thousands of hours are spent examining into dead records, looking at strange, weird, and distorted pictures which attempt to depict spiritual things by spurts of color or light. Strange symbols of writhing serpents and malformed beasts intrigue the human thought. *Prana* is much more stimulating than breath. Why? And so and so ...

Well, "Little children, let no man deceive you." We have wandered into a far country, and what have we found there but the inventions of the human mind, many of them fearful and terrible to behold — and not the least of them is the invention of war.

Sometimes a secret formula is given to a very special person, and it is claimed that unless this preparation is taken in connection with the study of Truth, the body-temple will not respond. Poor Jesus—He unfortunately didn't have any of the secret formulae with which to intrigue students. He had the simple revelation of a man's own soul, which could grasp a goblet of water in its hand and turn it into wine or into the elixir necessary to antidote "any deadly thing."

Yes, there is also the diet and the vitamin thing which comes along too, and everything is right for every man; but it is all written in the Bible, and the children who ate nothing but starch and water for days and days were fairer of flesh than those who had been upon the specially prepared diet of the king's table. But I do not presume to argue. When you bless the food that is set before you, *if you know what I mean*, it is then just exactly what should be taken into your system.

Can you grasp what I am saying? You are told to "eat what is set before you" in the name of Jesus Christ. Do you know what that means, and do you have a faint idea what it will do to food? Do you know that blessed food is always enough for no matter how many sit at the board—or do you? Do not try it, but just *do* it—and don't tell anyone, for no one will believe you, and you cannot prove it. But there it is for you, if you can *read* it … but … well, anyway, I am writing you much between the lines, and the blessing of it all is with you *now* as you read. It will be to every man who reads. Do you hear?

You wouldn't go out to clamor with the midnight darkness, would you—or would you? You wouldn't try to convince anyone, would you, or even call their attention to this power?

> Your business is to *let* your Light so shine; and when you do this, if—*if*—they see It and see It strongly enough to call upon you for It—you will release It in an overflowing stream of substance to them.

Chapter XIII

No Competition

The race is not to the swift ...

As long as the idea of competition exists in the mind of man, just so long will he believe that God and prayer are instituted for the purpose of competing with a negative power called evil.

Come out from the vicious circle of human wisdom (which is foolishness in the eyes of God) and be free. You have been laboring under such false beliefs as, "Competition is the life of trade," and quite naturally trade is the core and center of life as the human mind knows it. Yet are you told, "Come out from among them and be ye separate."

"If ye be in the Spirit, ye are no more under the curse of the law." And what, pray tell, is the curse of the law but the competition which causes you to "earn your living by the sweat of your brow." That is competition. But still "the race is not to the swift," and the race is not to the person who has been in "truth" for ages. That doesn't mean anything, since you could have died on the lap of Jesus, just the same as on a sick bed.

The ceaseless effort to find your place in the sun or to "get into expression" shows that you have fallen away from the one God and have entered into the competitive state of things, entered into the idea that you are a creator on your own. In Oneness, Wholeness, and changeless Spirit, there is no competition. There is nothing competing with you for your place, for *your* place is unique and different from every other manifestation in the universe.

When you see this, the struggle is over, and you begin to move from glory to glory instead of trying to hold your place in the sun or making a living. In the relative world, before a man realizes it, another has come along and taken his place, or at least is crowding him for his place. What a lovely picture—and what a heavenly thing to have created, and especially to have called "good" and "very good." What say [you]?

From cradle to grave, man "born of woman," born of the human belief, has his days "full of trouble" and naturally, *few*. He has the same thing as had Jesus, the carpenter of Nazareth; but when he begins to sense, even in a remote way, the Life substance, or the Life of Jesus the Christ, he begins to experience the "something" which takes him out of the competition of life.

It is more than amusing to hear a man stand and give thanks for the puny demonstration of health over a given disease, while in another part of his body he may be yet experiencing all sorts of evils. Yes, it is tragic; and we are faced with the plain facts of the case.

Do you believe? Do you? If you do, "open your eyes and receive your sight!" This line of reasoning

No Competition

probably annoys you, and you come back with the reply that you have "tried." But I told you *not* to try; and so again and again the idea of no-competition comes to you.

I have heard a person give a testimony which was almost maudlin with gratitude because he had been permitted to get a job, hard though it might have been, to earn his living. Yes, and that too by the sweat of his brow.

Well, "Ye do not need to fight," and yet here is one who is glad because God lets him have a job? Well, what is the matter? "I was in a line of fifty men, and I got the job." Is not that competition? And where is the revelation which says plainly that you are to go forth without thought for the purse, scrip, robe, etc., etc.? Do you hear?

Who are you?

All the going and coming on the mental plane avails nothing; it is all in the realm of competition. And presently you will understand that You — not you, but You — were sent forth into expression, and with you was sent the substance to carry out every idea which was necessary for you to bring forth the kingdom of heaven here and *now*.

Hard to believe; but then if you are following Christ, you will soon learn that everything He said and did was hard to believe and impossible for the human, competitive, thought-taking mind. Can you walk on the water — by any thought-process whatsoever — or increase the loaves and fishes? Well, if you cannot do these by taking thought, then you cannot understand what is meant by the "no-competition" idea; but it is wonderful if you can glimpse it. I wish you could. It is so glorious to begin even in a small degree to *sense-feel* what Jesus was giving to the universe.

God, to most metaphysicians, is here only to be proven. So funny—why should not God get tired of little mortals trying to *prove* Him? Wouldn't you, after about a thousand years, get tired of a lot of beetles in a slippery glass bowl, trying to get out? Think it over!

I have known so many "worthy" people to whom God paid no attention and so many "unworthy" people who seemed to prosper. I wonder why? Doesn't seem fair, does it—or does it?

A lady who had spent her life in the service of God wound up by living on a diet of graham crackers and hot water. She had given everything. Well, as the longshoreman brother said about her, "Tain't fair, tain't, and I should know; I have done everything and still can put away a good meal." Well, "Tain't fair, and so tain't," but what are you going to do about it?

Coming into alignment with the simple teaching of Jesus Christ will carry you out onto the stream of Life, where the Sodom and Gomorrah of human thinking will not bind you any longer. It is wonderful, the freedom it brings. The sense of individual superiority vanishes because you realize for the first

No Competition

time that but for the circumstance in which you happened to find yourself, you might have committed any and all of the crimes which you think are so terrible.

So what do you do when you realize this truth? Do you rush the Magdalene to the edge of the city and stone her to death, or do you give forth such a Light and Revelation that perhaps she may find some way out of the mistake, which you might have committed but for the grace of God? What do you do? Draw back your holy robes? Or do you feel the glorious compassion of Jesus, "Neither do I condemn you."

Just what do you do? Answer me. Do you make a reality of evil in one instance and not in another? Or do you "speak the Word," which might (I said might) release another, bound in the competitive world of earning a living by the sweat of her brow.

Don't ever say, "Well, I wouldn't do that," for that will surely be your move. That is the law of human thought and nature: "When I would do good, I do evil, etc." So watch and watch, and come to Me across the waters, if you can make it to the boat of Manifestation, and there will be no further competition for you.

With this lovely consciousness of no competition, you will see a thousand barriers swept away from you. You will see the difference between the mental and the spiritual planes of life. The mental plane can do many of the things which the spiritual does, but there is no reality in them.

You did not come here to compete with anybody, for you are an original idea in the Mind of God, and you have with you a complete *mise-en-scéne* [stage setting] against which to cast your shadow of expression. No one else knows the unique thing which causes you to be different—for you are peculiar and different—and it is just this peculiarity and difference which makes you an eternal success in Life. Understand—the people of God are "a peculiar people."

Beloved! Do you hear what I am saying unto you? "When the inspiration of the Almighty has come unto you, It will lead you into all things." Do you hear? When the inspiration of Jesus Christ has come unto you—and it comes the moment you *believe* in Him—just at that moment it comes! Wonderful, isn't it? Do you want to continue in your own imaginations, or will you come under this flood of inspiration which will make of your dull, drab life a flaming original thing that will ensure your success without competition?

A thousand men could come with the identical message that Jesus gave to the world and every one of them be so different as to attract to himself the crowds that Jesus attracted—it just seems I must tell you, Beloved, that you are about to see this thing, or else you wouldn't be reading this line.

Asking for favors, begging for a job whereby to sustain yourself, claiming your right with a fierce sense of human thought will get you no more than it got the practitioner who said she would work it out, even if she had to sleep in the park and eat carrots. She did both of these things, and yet the Lord seemed to have no pity on her.

Looking to another, copying his words or ideas, only makes you a dull imitation. I told you to "come out from among them and be separate." And when I say "separate," I mean just that. What do *you* mean, and what do you propose to do about it?

I don't care what this other has done or where he has gone. That will do nothing for you. Jesus said, "Go thou and do likewise," and that is exactly what will happen to you; for you will suddenly see that He offered you a no-competition path of attainment, knowing that every man had his own glorious expression and that this individuality and originality would keep him free from the terrible competition of the human life.

You, when you discover it, are the *Word of God*, and this Word is not subjected to the word of man or the words of man.

As the Word of God, you cease to come under the law and the curse of the law of competition. You are "sent," and either you hear this and step out and "come to me" across the waters of human belief or else you sink. Beloved, you are not competing with anyone. You have the lovely sense of Life within you, and this dispels the sense of health which has the limitation of sickness.

If "I have a way ye know not of," then why will ye doubt the possibility of the "no-competition" coming into manifestation in your life? "Go in and possess the land" does not suggest competition, does it?

"Take off your shoes; this is holy ground." Suddenly we see that the hobnailed shoes of human reason and belief are not fit to tread the inner courts of the Lord; so leave your understanding and follow Me. "Leave all and follow me." Do not go a-whoring after other gods if you do not want the results to follow, for the results are competition and strife. Do you hear?

You know what you are doing, don't you? You are just buying back the birthright that you sold for a mess of pottage. You sold your birthright, that lovely thing which had all the glorious powers which were manifested in Jesus Christ, that glorious thing which is so filled with Light that it could light every man unto salvation. Yes, that is what you sold for the mess of pottage that was offered you as an adequate return and that has proven to be a cauldron of human beliefs.

Well, "Jack and the Beanstalk," over which you have smiled and lifted your sophisticated eyebrows many times, sold a perfectly good cow for a hatful of beans; and you sold your birthright for a mess of pottage. And now you are beginning to understand that you were taken advantage of and that you want it back—and you are beginning to understand that you still have a chance to get it back!

Chapter XIV

No Weapon Shall Prosper

No (not any) weapon that is formed against thee shall prosper.

The law stands, and no combination of human inventions shall prevail against it; even the "gates of hell" shall melt and run as water. When you actually begin to understand the Jesus Christ Consciousness, you see something that is not written in the pages of history but which is impressed on the consciousness. It is a stepping-up into the next dimension, where all the beliefs and the wisdom of man are foolishness, no matter how wonderful they may seem to man.

The weapons that are formed against thee are many and vicious, and they include not only the sharp steel and the blunt bullet but all the savage jealousy and hatred and revenge of man; yes, even unto the beliefs in sickness and death. There are many *inventions* worked out by man, and many weapons formed against thee.

There is little escape in the human thought, but there is a free and beautiful immunizing influence with you the moment you step up into your Godhead. If a child can do this, so can you. Don't imagine it is difficult. The moment anything "hard" enters into the manifestation of Truth, you are traveling on the human pathway of defeat. Everything worthwhile is hard to the human thought, but nothing is hard to Me, and when you enter into this Consciousness of Jesus Christ, you will find that the statements of Jesus are laws which cannot be refuted by *any* beliefs of the human thought.

But how, says John Smith, can the invisible Spirit be immune to the leaden bullets and the keen edge of the weapons of human warfare? The only answer is, "It cannot." You see, or else you are still asking questions. You believe in the principle of Jesus Christ, who said, "Look again"—or you do not. The time-space of four months was approximated. Can you explain it? Can anyone? Not anyone, for it is above the human reasoning or intellect or even the human science or "inventions." There is no use talking about it. Either you see, or else you are still wishing, guessing, or trying to explain an equation which has no symbols or signs other than "shades, shadows, and linear perspective."

In other words, do you believe in Jesus Christ—the very one who withered the fig tree; who walked on the water; who caused the harvest to appear immediately and the water to turn into wine? Or do you believe in some old shaky human proposition which says that none of this can or will be done and in a burst of generosity says, "Well, show me, and I will believe"?

It is to laugh, to imagine that God is going to waste one moment trying to convince the curious.

What difference does it make whether or not the greatest erudition is convinced? It can never be convinced through the understanding of the human mind. There is nothing in the science of man which can approximate the fourth-dimensional teaching of Jesus Christ, and it is only when you enter into this Consciousness that you can and will transcend the foolishness of man's wisdom.

It is when you accept this revelation of Jesus Christ that you see why it is that "no weapon that is formed against thee shall prosper." Not any—do you begin to feel how it is—because you are "hid with Christ in God?" You have entered into the consciousness of your true Self and are stepped-up out of the human limitations of the John Smith who is so mutable and so easily destroyed by the weapons which are formed against him.

You will begin presently to understand that we are not bringing to you a new religion but a deep revelation, and this will certainly put the seal of silence on your lips, and you will go within and give thanks, as Jesus did when He said, "Thank you, Father; I knew all this was done, but I said thank you so that *they* would know something had taken place." It is so glorious, for in the midst of human warfare you will be delivered, and the cloak of invisibility will be thrown about you. You are "hid with Christ in God."

All sorts of wonderful and strange things will happen to you the moment you find your true identity. "They shall bear thee up in their hands, lest thou dash thy foot against a stone" means something more than the poetry of the 91st Psalm. It means an actual, literal experience that could and would take place in your life—for gravity, cohesion, adhesion, etc., are laws which do not function in Spirit. Nothing is hard to God—and nothing is impossible. And no man shall or can understand it, for it is "past finding out." It is not something that you *understand* through the human thinking but something that you *feel-sense* with the new dimension of your consciousness.

"No (not any) weapon that is formed against thee shall prosper." It is such a wonderful law, for it is so true and may be so provable in your daily life in the body of John Smith. Jesus made it clear that He could sidestep any of the laws of humankind. He moved instantly through the crowds, was instantly on the other side of the lake, could call forth twelve legions of angels and stop the farce of His crucifixion, and in a hundred ways stopped the silly functioning of the make-believe laws of the human thought. So, "no (not any) weapon which is formed against thee shall prosper."

This means any and all weapons, whether they be the leaden bullet or the keen, sharp edge of the enemy's sword. Not a single one of them can or will penetrate the armor of Spirit with which you are clad, until you see fit to "let" them come into manifestation by believing in them.

And yet this is nothing to boast about or to demonstrate. It is an accepted state of consciousness which will cause the sharpest steel to be blunted into the most useless piece of pig iron and cause the most deadly bullet to burst into fine powder. All this is recorded for you, and you will understand, or else you will ask, "But how?" There is no answer. Either you sense-feel this new dimension of Life or else you are still working with the idea that you can "demonstrate" or "know the truth" about it.

This is not the "demonstration." It is the already perfected state of consciousness that has gone before you and prepared the place of recognition for you, and it is the force which immediately dispatches you through the crowd of evil beliefs or puts you on the other side of the lake, away from all human argument and wonder. It is wonderful, and you—even you—are now ready to step up into this Consciousness and appropriate the wonderful revelation given to us by Jesus Christ.

Once you have entered into this revelation of the protection of the Presence, you see that it goes deeper and deeper into life and weeds out even the lesser "weapons" which have been formed against thee.

"Every tongue that is raised against thee shall be put to shame." It says *every* and not some, and it means just that. The moment you enter into the path of the Jesus Christ Consciousness, every evil tongue that is raised against thee shall be put to shame and shall presently be withered away as the fig tree.

Sometimes it seems a bit drastic that the fig tree should have been withered away; but after all, if it would give nothing forth, "why cumbereth it the ground?" And if the evil-minded human thing is busy about nothing but the destruction of the righteous, why should it cumber the ground? So the word goeth out, "Why cumbereth it the ground?" and this cleansing word will clear the terrain of all the evil things which have fashioned weapons against thee, either actually or literally.

"Clad in the panoply of Love"—clad in the armor of the revelation of Jesus Christ—you are impervious to any of the shafts of human thought, whether expressed or unexpressed. You have within you the power to wither the fig tree, and certainly you have within you the power to wipe clear the ground of your universe from the opposing forces of human thought.

It makes no difference how much mortal mind is inconvenienced, how it is confounded, dumb-founded, confused, or put to flight. Enough to know that you are "about your Father's business," and it is time *now* that you sensed your power and were able to put to flight the evil thing which comes at you. It shall come at you in one way and shall flee in ten, glad if it can escape the destruction or the withering influence of the Presence.

You have put up with enough of the human confusion and the human supposed power; now comes the actual consciousness that *"no* (not any) weapon that is formed against thee shall prosper," and therefore you are secretly immune from it all, no matter what the type or pattern of the weapon.

Yes, the sharpest steel shall be reduced to pig iron, ready again for the refiner's fire, and this carries right through the whole category of weapons which may be formed against thee.

Yes, "ten thousand may fall" and so and so, but it (the human weapon) shall not come nigh thee—because—and so if you understand what it means, you will know how it is that ten thousand may fall, and yet you pass through unscathed. Not because you are trying to prove anything but because you are in the Consciousness where "none of these things move" or touch you. It is wonderful, and you shall sing a song within your heart, even though you be in the fastness of the battle.

"How wonderful are thy blessings, O Lord!" How wonderful are the blessings which are streaming down about you even now, as you go forth through the waters which "shall not quench thee" and through the fires which "shall not burn thee," and you come out of the waters dry, and you come out of the flames without the smell of fire. It is all so above words, and yet you understand how it is that "I am with you always," even unto the end of your experience,

No Weapon Shall Prosper

and *I* shall lead thee by thy right hand into the place of glorification.

Any ground you stand upon is holy ground the moment you realize you are in the Presence. Any cup of cold water turns into the elixir of Life. You have with you everything that is necessary to bridge any human limitation if you but know the Presence and recognize that It is expressing through you at this instant, doing those wonderful and terrible things which the human mind cannot grasp.

Suddenly you know you are immune to the weapons that have been fashioned against you, and so you are free to help another not quite so fortunate. You can reach out; you can lift up; you can make whole; and you, in the beautiful, secret way of your consciousness, can do that which cannot be done.

Do you hear, Beloved, what is being said to you as I write it to you now? I know that you, thousands of miles away, will come upon it one day, and the wonderful burst of Light and illumination will come with it, and you will pause and say, "My Lord and My God." And suddenly you will arise and steal silently away into our lovely new day of expression. You will no longer tarry in the place of trying to make others see or understand—you will reveal. You will be and you will prove the Light of God without an effort.

"No weapon that is fashioned against thee shall prosper." Do you hear? Do you believe? No matter whether it be the actual knife and bullet or the sharp and cunning mechanisms of the human thought. The "snare of the fowler" shall catch only the fowler but not thee; and the one who has dug a hole shall fall into it.

> "No weapon
> (not any, do you hear?)
> that is fashioned against thee
> shall prosper." Selah.

Chapter XV

If Any Man

If any man will come after me, let him deny himself, and take up his cross, and follow me.

This invitation to follow after Me carries with it the ability to take up the "cross," which is the power to "x" out all the beliefs and appearances of beliefs under which man has labored so long.

The recognition of this Presence, this Trinity (in unity), Son-Father-Holy Ghost, enables man to deny himself the double-eyed, double-principled, thought-taking consciousness and follow Me. The more you look into this invitation the more you see hidden away in it.

"If any man will come after me. ... " If you are going to "go thou and do likewise," you will have to deny all the limitations of the present consciousness, all the wisdom called by God "foolishness," and learn of Me. This denying is not in any sense of the word a lip service to be carried out with denials. Declaring the nothingness of something is the greatest way in the world to make that "nothing" something, and trying to create a vacuum by denials is attempting something which both nature and God abhor.

It is a fact that a vacuum in consciousness cannot be—it can be created only in human belief. But when the recognition comes that this vacuum is already filled with the "substance of things hoped for, the evidence of things not seen," then you begin at once to understand the revelation of the unseen.

The "look again" is the extension of the double-eyed sight to a point where it becomes a far-visioned, single eye, able to see the flower before the seed and hear the answer before the question. In fact, when the eye becomes single, the whole body, or temple, is filled with light, and this single eye is the pure recognition of *God* in everything.

This recognition, as has been stated, is not a mental thing. It is something that has come after you are convinced within yourself that God is omnipresent. After that, your ability to bring this into manifestation depends on the "praying without ceasing" and the denying or disregarding of the vacuum which human thinking has created in your conscious mind and called by some evil name.

All evil is a vacuum in the consciousness of man. It exists, as has been said, only in belief. It cannot be communicated unless it is accepted by another. This vacuum, which seems so real, can be instantly filled with God; in fact, it has always been filled with God, awaiting recognition. The moment you see this simple teaching of the Master, the substance of God will appear in your consciousness where the vacuum of evil now stands.

Money, health, happiness are impersonal ideas when translated into Spirit, just as electrical heat, sound, and so forth all become just electricity when translated into their original form. Do you then begin to understand that "the substance of things hoped for, the evidence of things not seen" is there in the vacuum of human belief, waiting to be recognized as the very thing which is apparently causing the vacuum?

This extension of the vision into a single eye, the all-seeing eye of Spirit, gives you the ability to see through these vacuums of belief and discover that "the fields are ripe with harvest" at the very instant that you are, on the human reasoning plane, assuring me it will take four months before this can happen.

None of these marvelous things can come to pass so long as you *try* to make them happen; they must and will appear when you *see through* the vacuum of human belief and deny it by your recognition of the Presence, not by some word formula.

Do you begin to grasp this extended vision, the eye becoming single and you being able to see through the vacuum of belief? You are no longer fooled by the testimony which is stacked up in favor of evil, though it may have caused ten thousand to believe in it as real.

When you discover any lack in your life that is a vacuum, or a belief in the absence of God, then you can only deny it by complete indifference to all the history of its case. It is nothing as a vacuum, but this *nothing* is not stayed upon. Jesus, the Wayshower,

That Ye Might Have

spent no time trying to argue with the appearances of the barren field. He looked through it, through all time elements, and brought to light not the impersonal substance of Life, but the materialization of that substance.

Looking for things, for your good, for your happiness, with the double eye, you have the pairs of opposites with which to contend. You have money and poverty; you can see either or both with the double eye, and more likely you will see poverty, for under the race-consciousness, evil is so much more possible than good and so much more readily accepted. "Just my luck" is common talk in the streets of life. Nearly everybody accepts it as true. "Just my luck"—which is eternally evil.

So the double eye sees double—sees good and evil, sees past and future;—but the single eye, which has rid itself of all the beliefs *of* and *about* God and has accepted only the *One*, the Three in One, begins to experience the new dimension which says, "Before you ask, I will answer." In other words, look through the vacuum of human belief and discover the substance of the thing hoped for and call it into being.

All this lovely new dimension is presented with simplicity and naturalness, yet if it is reduced to the thought-taking plane, it is utter rubbish. There is nothing but foolishness to it all. It is only when the eye has become single—that is, when you have discovered there is *one God*—that you are able to "follow Me," and it is then that you can take up the cross, the power which crosses out all false beliefs by seeing through their vacuum.

To the personal sense, when the lack, disease, or unhappiness is discovered to be a mere vacuum, the inrush of manifestation is so instant that it is acclaimed a miracle.

It is acclaimed something supernatural, yet it was there all the while or else it never could have been made visible. Creation was completed and finished in six days and called *finished and done*—and *good*. There is nothing that can be added to it or taken from it.

Man was told to rest on the seventh day, which is *this day* we now live in. But the human consciousness, having been separated from its parent stem, began the tedious and terrible job of recreating the entire universe out of the chaos and darkness of human night, and it has continued to labor to make appear, by its slow-thinking process, that which has always existed here and *now*.

Jesus comes and declares again that it is done—completed and finished—and asks man in a free, easy manner to "take up this crossing-out power" and "follow after me."

Following after Me must not be confused with a personal Jesus in Jerusalem. This Me which you are to follow is the Father within you, and He gives you the ability to take up the crossing-out power and to follow after Him. This bringing everything down to the You of yours is perhaps a bit difficult, for we are inclined to pin all this wonderful thing on another so that, in the event it does not work for us, we can blame another instead of standing up to the failure ourselves.

"Mine eyes have seen the glory of the coming of the Lord." The single eye that is beginning to look through the vacuum of belief has already seen the coming into manifestation of this Lord. It is not disturbed and frustrated at every turn of the road and is no longer held in the hypnotic sway of human belief.

"Mine eyes have seen." Do you know what that means? It means looking through the letter and seeing the Spirit, for the letter of itself is dead and it killeth, but the Spirit quickeneth and maketh alive; and so this "mine eyes have seen" has a great possibility of correcting all the crooked vision, literally and figuratively, and the distorted images created by the thought-vision are discovered to be perfectly normal and beautiful.

As one looking in a concave or convex mirror is undisturbed by the distorted reflections, knowing their unreality, so the eye that is "seeing the glory" not only sees nothing but the Truth but is able to reflect it. "Awake thou that sleepest, and Christ shall give thee light"!

Do you hear? Do you *see* this light, actually and figuratively, in everything? It is the seeing with the single eye that gives the apperception of this light. It enters into everything past, present, and future, wipes out all the barriers and limitations, and disintegrates the vacuum.

Do you understand now how a glance can heal, just as can a touch? Do you begin to see the power that Jesus knew was indigenous in every man? Do you begin to extend the dimension of sight and appropriate all of its offices? It can heal with a glance, *if you can,* but this must not be done with effort. Staring is not a glance; fixing the eyes in a hypnotic gaze is not glancing.

Glancing is light, natural, spontaneous. It is filtering through the vacuum of a belief and lighting up the reality. And as it *glances* at this reality with the power of *sight,* another also may perceive the truth and be instantly healed. For the "virtue goes out" in the glance. Even as Jesus perceived that "Some *one* has touched me," when He had been crowded about all day, so will you perceive that some one glanced at you or you glanced at some one, and "it" took place.

All this is such foolishness in the eyes of human intellect. But we are not concerned with that. We are following after Jesus Christ, and the infinite care with which we go into it makes it all sacred and holy and too precious to be "cast unto dogs."

The single eye that has enabled you to "read" what is said directly to you by Spirit, to accept without equivocation or limitation, is the actual entering into the New Day wherein the former things are passed away. Behold, all things become new. It is wonderful!

Mine eyes have seen the glory of the coming of the Lord—the glory, the glowing rays of light going out in all directions from the center of your being, the Lord in the midst of you.

This extended vision which sees everything you have done when "under the fig tree" is not to be brought to pass in order that you may be a psychic or a fortune teller, but that you might see how to go into the kingdom and that you might see through the vacuums of the human mind and bring reality to pass by revelation.

You are a revelator, and you have the clear vision to such degree as you can accept the words of Jesus Christ, to the degree they are your own. You are the temple through which this wonderful thing must come into being. You are the Light that is to light every man (in your world) unto salvation. You are the Light which cannot be hid, set upon a hill.

All these things are true of you when you have made this union of body and soul and have discovered the Father within; when you, with abandon, *take* the Word and return to Jehovah and there release Its fulfillment. *When you can, you can.*

Do you hear? Do you feel—see? If so, you begin to realize what is back of this gift of Jesus to you.

As sight becomes a pure, unadulterated spiritual quality, it begins to function for the first time in its new capacity. It is taken out of the limitation of muscles and nerves and is released into a field so large and infinite that one is lost in following.

Just think of it. You, you the former "worm of the dust," the one who was "born in sin and conceived in iniquity," have this glorious gift of vision—extended sight, single eye, sweeping like a great searchlight in all directions, into the past, into the future of the conscious mind—detecting all the mental and thought tie-ups that are acting as causes in your life today for the evil there manifested, and untying these thought patterns of yesteryears and preventing any future tangles because it *sees through*.

You will see through, or else you will drop down to the level of thought-taking and *try* to see through, in which case you will see nothing but the picture floating in the vacuum of the mental plane, for all the evil in your life is made and sustained by thought. Snap the thought and the picture must go. And so this seeing through the vacuum is another manner in which you are enabled to disintegrate the picture of evil.

You note the figurative angle of all the teaching of Jesus Christ. For instance, when He says, "If any man will come after me, let him take up his cross and follow me." Now, literally, to the consciousness this is impossible. Just what are you going to do with an imaginary cross? And then in an effort to make something out of it, you take up a thing called "burden," which immediately you identify as part of the life of Jesus. What good can come from this contradiction since Jesus said, "Cast your burdens on me, and I will sustain you"? And in another place He says, "Take up the cross and follow after me."

Do you begin to see, with this single eye, through the mystification that has arisen in human thinking and obscured the Light? Seeing the double standard, or the pairs of opposites, you immediately begin to feel sorry for Jesus; yet He did say, "I come that your joy might be full." How shall we interpret these contradictory things? There is an endless procession of utterly absurd commands if you take them from the conscious-thinking plane. They are not only impossible, they are worse. Yet every one of them is possible when the eye becomes single.

The glory of the new vision—"Mine eyes (single eye) have seen the glory of the Lord." I have seen Him in loathsome leprosy, in the most suffocating poverty, in the morass of futility. I have seen Him through all this vacuum, and He has answered, "Here am I; what will you?"

"Master, Master, Master!" and the little John Smith (the glorious temple of the living God) must at last recognize the triumph of Jesus Christ in the universe of belief.

Do you grasp how it is that you come again to the door of a consciousness and knock, and if any man "sees" your voice (yes, the senses merge into one) and opens unto you, you will come in to him and glance at him and he at you? And the former evil thing that has been floating in the vacuum of human thought will evaporate as a mirage on the desert, and there will appear, in its place, God, in whatever form necessary to accomplish the continued sense of heaven here and *now*.

Faint echoes of the Permanent Self, before it left its Garden of Eden, sound through the mists of matter. Often have you stood in a quandary of human confusion and have said, "Let me see, let me see," only to find yourself still in human darkness because you were using the double sight which had to look "through the glass, darkly" and could see only distortion and evil. But with this single eye which has again come to you through recognition of the Presence, you are able to see "face to face."

Isn't it glorious? *Then,* "through the glass, darkly" of the double sight which is the perpetual "overcomer," but *now,* "face to face." The *now* is the instant you can accept sight as a reality. You will see, and then it will turn into the lovely light-filled consciousness—"Behold." You are beholding, for the first time, God in His universe and are recognizing your part in the grand *man*ifestation—your place in the sun, your place in glory—because your eyes have become single, and the glory of *beholding,* instead of trying to "see," is accomplished with the strange new-dimensional power which can manifest what it beholds.

Out of the glorious eyes of you streams this spiritual sight, and this pouring through the temple drives from every niche and cranny the thieves of belief regarding your vision. Suddenly your eyes are opened, and the steady stream of light continually passes through, bringing with it a balanced perfection of sight.

If your "eyes" have seen the glory of the Lord through Jesus Christ, they will become single and filled with Light, and the former pictures floating on the vacuum of human belief will be no more. The mirage of poor vision will have passed into oblivion.

"Fear not ... stand and see the salvation of the Lord," which He will show you *today*.

"Can you see?" is the same as "can you take it?" Neither of these questions has to do with anything physical; the physical or the mechanics come later. The ability to *see* (or take) comes first, and then your eyes go through the necessary adjustment.

"Come and see a man who told my fortune," and the woman of Samaria missed *seeing* a man who was offering her "living waters" which, if she drank thereof, she would "never thirst again." *Never* means eternity, and yet the woman wanted to see a man instead of to *see* a *man*ifestation of the New Day.

Open your eyes! Behold
the glory of the New Day!

Chapter XVI

The Permanent Identity

The only impermanent thing in the universe is matter; it is so *immaterial* that it is ever disintegrating before your eyes. It is hardly entitled to the name solid, if that term is to convey anything lasting, for it is in a constant state of change. On this changing basis of life, man has tried to work out something that would endure, but before he can establish a foundation of this mutable, immaterial "stuff" that he calls matter and reality, it has so completely shifted its elements and changed its nature as to make anything but the most transient structure worse than useless. Hence the body, or temple, is allotted only seventy years, if it receives more than good care. Even seventy years is a long time, for it is beset with millions of manmade laws which are constantly working against it.

From the day the little temple is put on earth, it is weighted down with a thousand and one laws and "don'ts." It is so filled with fears and beliefs that its whole life is one long effort to fight a force called *evil*, or in more specific terms, *devil*, knowing all the while, it is playing a losing game. Sickness, misfortune, and disease stalk the land, and no matter what man does, or tries to do, he can find no exact remedy for it. What he finds works sometimes and fails at others. He is only a pawn of chance; and yet he is

That Ye Might Have

taught, along with all this fear, that he has some sort of power to fight this devil.

He discovers from the very start that he must hurry on to get an education so that he may earn a living, education being necessary to this end. When he takes his first position, he discovers he is working for a man who has had virtually no "book learning" but has made the grade without it and is remarkably clever at it. But if he tries to get along with but little education, the little "temple" finds that the first man he works for has a string of degrees after his name that virtually includes the whole alphabet, and his employer immediately explains that there is no use trying to make a living without a good classical education.

The whole changing, shifting thing is "a lie and the father of it," and the more one goes into its system of life, the more he finds he hasn't a leg to stand on.

Struggling through this quagmire, man suddenly hears that he must learn to "think right," be "healed" or "prospered," or something else; so he tries this and for the moment becomes drunken with the offers made by the various systems of new thought. But the little temple has only a very limited capacity of absorption, and the moment it has reached a point of saturation, it is through, and man dismisses it all by sighing, "It doesn't work anymore."

A few years ago, a noted French scientist set the world agog by giving it a very simple little affirmation with which to suggest that everything was all right

The Permanent Identity

and that each day increased this "rightness." The slogan ran through the world like a breeze of fresh air, and thousands could testify as to its efficacy; then it reached a point of saturation, and that was the end.

Cure-alls of every sort have been applied to man's misfortunes with some measure of success, but finally the old devil, futility, overtakes him; he sees there is nothing to any of it but *belief* and that as long as he can feed a belief with concentrated thought, he can in some measure sustain that picture in the universe.

Strangely enough, he can hold pictures of evil into place with comparative ease! It is much easier to be sick, sinning, fearful, poor than it is to be rich, happy, well, and so forth. Yet on Sunday, and perhaps other days, he makes prayers to a God whom he claims is All-present, All-powerful, and All-knowing.

No wonder such a confusion of ideas results in death. It is in accordance with the law. Anything evil can happen to matter, for it is "conceived in sin and born in iniquity" and is filled with the capacity for negative manifestations. Why? Because it is dying from the moment it has been conceived. It is rushing on as fast as it can to the grave. Why? Because it has lost its connection with the *One*. It is the rose cut from the parent stalk, and no matter how fresh it looks and how long kept fresh on ice or in water, it begins dying the moment it is cut from the bush.

And so man is gradually finding out that he is a dying manifestation and that hour by hour he is losing everything worthwhile in the manifest world. To offset this, he stacks up a huge fortune and fancies he is accomplishing something. But this fortune, too, is subject to every evil law and condition, and man has no rest and finally finds himself helpless while a flock of dogs and vultures pull the "body" of his estate to pieces, fight each other, sue each other, and sometimes kill each other for the filthy lucre of his accumulation.

It is not a nice picture to contemplate, but, at that, it is nothing new. You know it, have wondered at it many times, and then, because you could do nothing about it, have closed your eyes to it and said glibly, "I will not judge from appearances." Well, what you say doesn't make any difference. It is what one can do from the height of the revelation given by Jesus Christ that counts.

Jesus, the carpenter, came recognizing this shifting, impermanent nature of matter with all its foibles and fears, and to this He brought a panacea. He revealed the fact that man, created in the image and likeness of God, is given dominion over everything in the universe.

Whatever took place in the parable of the Garden of Eden was a matter of free will and choice on the part of the *Adam* (you) and your mate (*Eve*)—the knowing (Adam) and the feeling (Eve) elements of your make-up. And by this free will did you let yourself out of the garden into a world of the manifestation of

The Permanent Identity

separation. In other words, you decided to go it on your own, and accordingly you separated yourself from your Permanent Identity, since which time you have wandered through all sorts of characters and worlds and lives, carried on by the impetus of your desire.

But as the energy of this desire was spent, man saw no source from which to draw a fresh supply, and so, after eons of time, he began to look again for that which he had so foolishly forsaken. For a day or two, he has been doing this—the measure of Spirit being "a thousand years is but a day" but to the human thought, centuries.

When the discovery of your Permanent Identity is again made, you will find time rolling up as a scroll and vanishing, together with its strange and terrible history and all the false faces and masks, or personalities, you have worn.

Even now, you stand on the threshold of this New Day and are beginning to see how it is that the change in matter takes place. There are, as has been explained before, the three states—Son, Father, God. The Father and Son are *One*. God is the great universal Power in all and through all and which is stepped down into visibility through this hookup of Father and Son. Matter, the body with its changing thought, is suddenly fused with Spirit, the Soul, and "the Word becomes flesh." In other words, "matter" is changed into *flesh*. "Yet in my flesh shall I see God," and the transmutation immediately gives Spirit a chance to materialize Its desires and at the same time lifts the erstwhile "matter" condition into a level of consciousness where "the former things are passed away" and "shall not come into mind nor be remembered anymore."

Succinctly: the capacity to cognize evil as a power is completely deleted; there is nothing in the "flesh" or the resurrected temple-body which can or does contact or permit a contact with the former belief in evil.

In the absolute, flesh cannot manifest disease. It has not the capacity to experience it. The limitations of human language cause us to use a word in many different ways, with as many meanings. *Flesh*, as we speak of it here, is the perfect manifestation of Spirit being "made flesh" and matter being made Spirit, a fusing of the two, just as yeast and flour finally are neither yeast nor flour, but are bread. So this flesh is that substance which is not capable of experiencing all the beliefs to which matter is heir. It has no capacity to earn its living "by the sweat of its brow," for it "does not live by bread alone, but by every word that proceedeth out of the mouth of God."

Everything is a contradiction in the recounting of this higher dimension, for, as previously noted, there is no language capable of expressing it.

> So when, by the same token, you exclaim in pure recognition of the universal God of all creation and the universe, "It is wonderful," it becomes pure recognition. It is calling the *Name-Nature* of God, and that Name-Nature always

responds, just as an obedient person answers when his name is called, and "the Word is made flesh," and your heaven becomes established on earth.

Do you begin to see why Jesus Christ came and was known as the *wonderful* one, the one of whom it had been said, "His name is Wonderful, Mighty, the Everlasting, and of his reign there shall be no end"? Because this very matter-Spirit, Spirit-matter, or the Word made flesh, is the Savior of you and your world. It is then wonderful, and at this name every knee shall bend in recognition of the priceless revelation.

Jesus met each situation with an *apparent* carelessness, a disregard for appearances, which was disarming and sometimes incited men to anger, just as many people today are angry when their evil is not recognized as something and when it is treated for what it really is—a crystallized belief in a power apart from God. The very thing they wish to get rid of they also wish to have accepted as real. If it is not made enough of and they are not able to elicit a lot of pity, they will go elsewhere, not realizing that every bit of sympathy for evil (any misfortune) they pull out of the universe only intensifies the condition they are trying to get rid of. Don't proclaim that it is all a belief and nothing and in the next second waste endless arguments trying to prove that it is terrible and real.

This Permanent Identity stands at the door and knocks, but It does not force an entrance, and

That Ye Might Have

It does not go in to cure, to heal, or to save; yet in another way It does all of these things. It goes in to reveal what is eternal and changeless; and this revelation, if it is accepted by the matter consciousness, is able to show forth the perfect manifestation, absorbing the thought which has been sustaining the former evil.

Jesus Christ, standing at the door of any consciousness, even though it is experiencing "death," is unmoved and untroubled. "Behold, I stand at the door," and with this flesh consciousness; with this knowledge of the Permanent Identity, I stand and stand and *stand;* and as the light pours through into manifestation, the evil melts and disappears, and with it, its manifestation.

When you take a picture, you do all *you* can do for the moment. You recognize certain things definitely as real and true. You do not enumerate them. You automatically focus your camera on the picture you desire and photograph it as a reality. After that, you proceed to bring it forth through a developing bath. At first nothing is visible. And if you stop to judge from appearances or listen to the man "whose breath is in his nostrils," you will open the darkroom door and let in the daylight, which will ruin your entire effort.

Do you begin to see *what you are to see* in the individual when you stand at his door—consciousness? You do not create the picture. It is already there. You do not make him well or happy. You bring out, through the recognition of his Permanent Identity, the perfect picture, the picture "shown to you on the mount," which is eternal and passeth not away.

And this is the thing that takes place in the revelation of Jesus Christ. He is able to make this recognition, and if man can accept it and does not open the darkroom door of unbelief, it immediately changes the body and brings about the thing called healing. Yet, in reality, there is no healing, for impermanent matter cannot be healed or cured.

"Yet in my flesh shall I see God." "No man shall see my face and live." No matter-man can look upon the brightness of this Consciousness and live any longer in the utter darkness of his limitations and separation from his Creator. He dies the moment he comes in contact with that revelation as given by Jesus Christ, and from that time on he dies daily to the evidences of matter, as he sees more and more of this Permanent Identity.

"Heaven and earth are full of thee." The whole universe is of God, the substance from which all things must and do appear, and there is no place or location into which you may go that this glorious substance is not instantly available. This becomes true only when you stop "using" it as something apart from you. Otherwise, you presuppose it to be a supernatural power which works for you only on certain occasions, perhaps once in a lifetime.

Any time you touch My robe or even the hem of My garment, something is bound to happen, but to put on the whole seamless robe, you must follow after the Master, Jesus Christ, straight into the flesh state of life. Believing, accepting, making it ever more and more natural, simple, and easy, and always with more and more divine indifference. Then is it *wonderful*, and the glory of it all fills you with such bliss that all other joys melt into nothingness, for you have come into *your* kingdom.

Behold, *you* stand at the door. You stand with the lovely "flesh" consciousness, which will not descend to the level of sympathy but will stand in compassion, waiting, and always with divine indifference, seeing with the single eye all pictures of evil disintegrate with the coming into being of this Permanent Identity.

If, however, the door on which you knocked remains closed and will not be opened, then "what is that to thee?" You have accomplished your part of the glorious thing. You have brought the gift of the true picture of man's Permanent Identity, and if it is rejected, "shake the dust (of the rejection) from off your feet," as so often did Jesus, and go your way. There can be no backward thinking of what "might have been" or any condemnation or sitting in judgment; you let it pass into oblivion. There are yet other doors which will gladly open and where you can stand and deliver. "Raise the dead." "Heal the sick."

Stand at the *door* and contemplate
the Permanent Identity.

Chapter XVII

Evolution and God

Everything evolves but God. He is changeless, eternal in the heavens (consciousness) and fadeth not away.

Matter is the shadow of Spirit cast through the "glass, darkly" into a self-created state of things. It is constantly changing and shifting and has for a foundation evolution. The belief goes so far in some schools of wisdom as to posit the origin of its present-day degree of perfection in the amoeba or a bit of protoplasm. But since every mortal man is "a liar and the father of it," what difference does it make what it says about the origin or composition of matter?

When the revelation of the Almighty comes to you, it shall lead you into all things and cause you to *see* that with the removal of rose-colored specs the rose-colored horse becomes white—or rather, is white and always has been white—and that nothing was done to the horse. Likewise, when you begin to step up into your Permanent Identity and understand who you are, you will be able to remove the "glasses" from the sick man and cause him to see that his body is well instead of covered by a pattern of disease and fear.

As you begin to grasp just what is going on, you will understand a thousand and one laws of Jesus

That Ye Might Have

Christ. You will see how it is that you do not need to "take thought" of the purse, robe, ring, or passport. You will understand why it is that you can give to every man that which he asketh, for you are not looking any more through the "glass, darkly" of human thought, but are come to the place of your true Self. You are only revealing to a sick man that he was and is created "in the image and likeness" and given dominion over everything on, over, and under the earth; to cause him to drop the evolutionary idea of matter and enter into his Godhead and be saved. From what? His belief—and in the final analysis, saved from nothing.

It is said that the sower shall find his flower before the seed. So also he will find the bird before the egg and his good before he asks and countless other things too precious to mention. "Eyes have not seen, ears have not heard, neither hath it entered into the heart of man the things that are prepared for those that love the Lord." You know what you have already seen, and you know what you have already heard, and you know what manner of things have entered your mind, many of them lovely and wonderful—but they are nothing and are so far below the "things that are prepared" there is no comparison.

One flash, one moment of this recognition, wipes out the whole evolutionary pattern of the human mind, and the beggar with forty years' belief suddenly leaps into the air well, whole, perfect.

Yes, one glimpse of this glorious Truth, and the man born blind finds himself with glorious wide-open eyes, so instantaneously done that human reason and thought cannot approach it.

Chapter XVIII

But Why Should This Happen to Me?

During the last month, I have had half a hundred letters all asking the question, "But why should this happen to me?" or, "Out of a clear sky such and such a thing happened to me." And then the recitation of some pretty terrible happenings followed.

We are in the last days of the present regime, and the Spirit has troubled the muddy waters of human thinking and has brought up many ugly and unknown manifestations. Old karmic accounts, forgotten or never known, have been coming up for settlement. Also, they are coming up as a final push or urge to cause you to go farther into the Jesus Christ Consciousness—even so far as to come under Grace instead of remaining under the curse of the law.

We realize that part of the old human system, the Adam-consciousness, is the endless sowing and harvesting of evil, with the overtone of blessing in that it is supposed to bring you closer to God through suffering. Purification through suffering was the motto of the inquisitional days, when the more one was tortured the more godly he was supposed to be.

It goes without saying that many people through great suffering have turned to God; but in this turning, it was not for the love of God but for the desperate hope that some help could be gained. God does not have to seek worshippers through fear, for God is Love, and God is Spirit, and those that worship Him must so understand.

The idea of karma is quite in accord with the journey of the Adam-consciousness through the self-created universe of evil. It is one of the lesser-known laws and governs many of the things called chance and luck; and it finally has to be brought to the surface and dealt with if we are to enter into heaven.

Jesus was constantly neutralizing karmic laws and also offering a means of wiping the slate clean of all past evils, yet we have been so deaf and blind that we could not hear or see this means of escape. "Strong meat is for the strong man." So we subsisted on the "milk of the word"—overcoming and over-coming—but we failed to overcome the evil situation or belief and were overcome by it.

"A man's enemies are those of his own household" because they kill him with kindness. They know his weaknesses better than his strengths, and with their "love" they would save him from any experience. They know his weaknesses to such an extent and love him so much they would withhold everything from him, while actually believing they want to help.

They are sincere, so do not condemn. They mean well; but nevertheless, they are the "hometown" folks who will not accept a prophet who arises among them. Why? Because they know him—and especially his weaknesses. A strange prophet may come and bring all sorts of Light to them, but not the home prophet.

So the prophet, or you, begins to see how it is that the "good enemies" of your own household must be given their freedom if you expect to move into the new dimension of Light, remembering also that the very same quotation applies to the consciousness of the individual. The things that you have in your *own* mind can and will be enemies to your on-going, if the temple is not cleansed.

"Well, the evil has already happened to me. I have already paid but have suffered so tremendously from the injustice," etc.

What is the neutralizing power over the results of things we have already suffered? How do we remove the "smell of fire" which hangs to our garments in the form of resentment, injustice, even hatred?

The first thing necessary is to classify it as karmic debt. The actors in the drama of your evil were necessary to that stage of things. They could no more help themselves on that level of thinking than could Judas, so it is of little use to blame them. You have paid the price, however painful, and having paid this karmic debt, you are entitled to freedom from the smell of fire on your garments. You will never be able to cleanse the garments until you come face to face with the fact that those very Judases were necessary at that moment to force you up out of the existing state of affairs.

But Why Should This Happen to Me?

Jesus submitted to Judas knowingly. He was fully aware of the fact that He was no more under "the curse of the law," and He even mentioned the fact that He could at the last moment "call upon my Father and he would send twelve legions of angels." But He stepped down into the place of human fate and allowed the hateful pattern to have its way, in order to prove in the final analysis that it had no power.

Gradually you see that the very people and things which were apparently used against you were working for you. They have changed and broken up some old hard and set forms and allowed the Light of the next dimension to flow through. If you can release the self-pity from your Soul long enough to let the Light in, you will begin to understand in a new way why Jesus said, "Bless those who deceitfully use you," etc.

It is wonderful. You bless everything and everybody; and every time the faintest odor of the "smell of fire" comes to you from your garments, you begin the song of praise and blessings. You bless the whole thing right out of existence. The hard fast knots are untied, and the whole tangled situation goes free. This is not done in the holier-than-thou attitude of mind. It is done from the new elevation, for presently, "if ye faint not," you will come to the same place where Jesus stood and will have the option to "pick it up or lay it down" and will know that "no weapon that is formed against thee shall prosper," — and you will also know something about the withered fig tree.

Laws that are not written in any book and which are told only between the lines of Jesus' words are put in your hands, and you will know that "I have a way ye know not of" really means something. And you will then see how it is that Jesus came to annul the human fate and cause you to enter your Divine Destiny. You are in the world, but not of it. You are under the law, but not under the curse of it; and you are being equipped to go forth and actually help and heal the ones reaching out for Light, this time without all the back-kick that usually accompanies it.

And so, presently you will have washed your garments clean and will realize that the former things are passed away, yea, even the smell of fire of suffering and injustice and karmic debt which clung to you so tenaciously. And also you will begin to sense-feel that you have broken the old wheel of karmic fate and are entering into your Divine Destiny.

Chapter XIX

Nothing Hidden

*There is nothing that is hidden
that shall not be revealed.*

So runs the law, and "not one jot or tittle shall be removed until the law be fulfilled."

Everything you possess today was hidden at one time, and yet it has been revealed, perhaps through the slow processes of the human mind. The airplane, for instance, was "hidden" at the time of Jesus, yet it could have been revealed because everything of which it is composed was there then, just as it is here now. The only thing lacking was the recognition of it as an idea in the Mind of God. The moment we see this, we begin to understand how it is "there is nothing new under the sun" — and at the same time, "behold, I make all things new."

Revelation shall follow revelation, and miracle shall follow miracle because the floodtides of Spirit are now upon the world, and whosoever has open gates will receive the blessings in countless numbers.

The idea rests in the Mind of God, and when this is recognized, the embodiment begins to manifest. The mistake of man has been to try to force the issue or to try to fashion or create the thing he desired, instead of going back to his Godhead and finding the idea there, ready and waiting, hidden in God.

When once he finds it there, he can speak the Word of releasement, and according to his faith does it take on body and form, very much as if a matrix or form were placed in front of a hydrant. Immediately the form or mold is placed there, it begins to fill up, either instantly or drop by drop, according to the amount of water turned on, and while this illustration is ridiculous in the eyes of revelation, yet in a way it will give you a working basis.

First, you discover the Idea in the Mind of God, as Jesus went "unto my Father" and discovered the substance of bread and fish sufficient to feed five thousand. When He asked the Father, or recognized the Idea as already in the Mind of God, He then was able to bring it into manifestation, and in His state of consciousness, He could literally precipitate it—sidestep the time-space element of human thought which says, "You say it is four months to the harvest; I say, look again."

Whether you can do it instantly or whether by a slower method, you will begin gradually to understand that the Idea back of your desire rests eternally in the Mind of God, waiting, as it were, to be born, and because of this Idea in the Mind of God, you have the urge or desire to bring it forth. Every desire you ever have had was caused by the *Idea* in the Mind of God waiting to be born, but "through the glass, darkly" of human thought, many a terrible distortion has been brought forth, sometimes stillborn and sometimes nothing but "clouds without rain."

"Awake thou that sleepest, and Christ shall give thee Light. Awake and arise from the dead. There is no wisdom of man that is anything but foolishness in the eyes of God, and so any argument, guessing, or fooling around with psychological truths or affirmations or systems of truth is so much wasted time. Go within and find it. "Go in and possess the land" and find there the Idea in the Mind of God. This Idea, established as a reality in your mind, will have the stage set for the New Birth. Presently, you will find that it is beginning to take form and shape.

The form and shape, or the embodiment, of the Idea will depend entirely upon you. In the Mind of God is the Idea of abundance, but your present consciousness of abundance will determine the amount of wherewithal you will possess. To some, five thousand is a fortune; to others, a million is spending money. The degree, and even the quality, is entirely up to you.

The idea of a chair, for instance, is something upon which to rest. Naturally, it is not designated as any kind or shape, etc. The bringing out of this Idea is entirely up to the individual; hence, the hundreds of kinds of chairs we have.

Ideas in the unmanifest realm will be revealed as soon as you make your assumption and take your place in the Sun of Life. You are the Christ of God too, just as Jesus was, and this without taking one bit of power or reverence away from our Beloved One.

You are the Jesus or John Smith until you do as He did and discover your true identity. And then you become the manifest Christ, and you begin to bring forth into manifestation all the things the unmanifest Christ knew and experienced.

"When ye pray, believe that ye shall receive, and it shall be so." So when you contemplate God and discover the Idea there, perfect and whole, you are at the beginning of the New Revelation, the beginning of the appearance of the new pattern. And so surely as you appropriate that Idea in the Mind of God as real and eternal, so soon will you be able to "let the child be born"—to let the manifestation come into being.

You are the manifest Christ of God,
and it is your business
to be about your Father's business.

Chapter XX

The Year of Our Lord

To begin with, this is AD 19___. Fill the date in yourself. The place is always either heaven or hell, and the appointed hour is *now* or some dim, distant date. When you begin to realize that this (yes, this very hellish year) is the year of our Lord and that this hell you are living in is the kingdom of heaven, either you scream out in human helplessness, "Well, why doesn't it come to pass then?" or else you look the whole situation over and find that no year in your life has been more fiendish and that no place has ever been more like hell. Why, at the very moment you are thinking about it, you are literally consumed by the flames of evil of every sort, over which you seem to have no control whatsoever.

And yet it is "the year of our Lord," and it remains the year of our Lord through a thousand years of the devil until you rise to the consciousness that this is so. This rising to the consciousness is not stirring physically—nor yet trying to rid yourself of loathsome objects and people—but a sudden recognition, the same sudden kind that came to the beggar, forty years a cripple at the temple gate, when he leaped into the air and praised God; the same thing that causes the individual who has made his bed in hell to become conscious that *I* am here and to experience the change from evil to good without anything happening, but with much suddenly appearing.

It is all in consciousness, and consciousness is attained by being still and knowing that "I am God." Suddenly you see that it is so, that no matter whither you go, even unto the ends of the earth, there My right hand shall lead thee. Are you afraid where it will lead you? Dare you to come to Me across the waters? Dare you to stretch forth your hand?

All these questions and a thousand others will pass through your mind as you suddenly burst the bonds of the old human hypnotism and release the floods of "yea, Lord, I will." And suddenly you "leap into the air" with a song of joy on your lips because even as you appropriate this revelation, the year of the devil becomes the year of our Lord, and the kingdom of hell becomes the kingdom of heaven.

> And there is something in your heart which keeps pouring out the blessings on all mankind, and you are praying the prayer of breathless adoration, the praying without ceasing—"my Lord and my God."

Chapter XXI

I Will Not Let You Go

I will not let you go until you bless me.

So speaks Jacob after struggling all night with his problem. He had come through his labors in the darkness of human thought and reasoning, "but when the morning came" (when he had light to see his freedom as an established thing in Spirit), he was then ready to "loose him and let him go." He saw that irrespective of the hurt he had experienced, it had been self-inflicted. But it is interesting that in discovering this thing, he was not willing to let it go until it had blessed him. In other words, since he had gone through all the hallucination of evil and suffered for it, he intended to have something out of it. He demanded the blessing of having gone through the problem.

Going through the fire and coming out without the smell of fire on your garments is a grand thing, and one of the ways to get rid of the smell of fire, which does cling so many times after the fire, is to demand a blessing from the experience. This demanding is merely the finding out the why and wherefore of it all and seeing what was in the experience.

When you find that *only* good was in it after all (though this does not in any manner of the word intimate that going through endless experiences is good or part of God's plan), you automatically take away from the situation any remorse, revenge, hatred, or worry about getting even; and when you have done this, you have gotten the blessing from it, and it is dropped from consciousness and is forgotten, and the place thereof is no more. "Vengeance is mine; I will repay" relieves you of the very tedious and unpleasant duty of getting even with the one who has lent himself as a Judas in your life. Calling down the blessing is also calling down the fire and the Light which has its own way of bringing the revelation to all parties concerned—and without your personal supervision.

Prophecy

Let your thought dwell on this for a while, since the tree of meditation beareth wholesome fruit and he whose duty is to teach should set examples, though he know the answers, yet withholding them:

The dogs bark when the caravan moves on. The dogs fight when the caravan has gone. The caravan proceedeth and the dogs lick, each his own wounds, in the dust ("Tsiang Samdup" in *The Devil's Guard*).

It is so wonderful when you come to the place where you can demand, "I will not let you go until you bless me." What is this thing I have gone through? Why was I betrayed? Why did he do such and such a thing?" —and a thousand and one other questions—

for as soon as you enter into the equation in this fashion, you will find something taking place, a change and releasement from a bondage, and presently the smell of fire shall have disappeared from your garments.

When you call for freedom from a situation, remember that it must come in God's way, not yours. "My Son, despise not prophecy"—but be sure it is prophecy before you accept it. There is the gift of prophecy from the standpoint of spiritual illumination, and there is the spurious gift of fortune-telling, which is the residue of the Light strained through the veils of superstition, fear, and emotion.

Through the "glass, darkly" of mortal thinking, every sort of distorted idea comes into manifestation, filled with chaos and evil. "Who can, by seeking, find out God?" Then what human mind is in position to prophesy, since "no man knoweth what a day may bring forth." And yet there is the gift of prophecy.

The gift of prophecy is able to see the natural outcome of a chain of events in the human illusion and also to see what is necessary to sidestep the fulfillments of these events. A bud that is destroyed puts an end to the manifestation which might have grown into an enormous branch, and so, with the understanding of Jesus Christ, man is enabled to destroy the buds of evil human things before they have time to come into fruition.

The gift of prophecy is not turned on and off like a hydrant. It is exactly what it says—it is a gift, and a gift is always given. And so the gift of prophecy is given to the prophet at the precise moment it is needed to throw illumination on some darkened entanglement of human thought, and for no other reason.

Thousands of prophets (so-called) today are using or attempting to use this gift for the purpose of frightening people into being good or into adhering to some personal doctrine. "Where there be prophecies, they shall fail."

The gift of prophecy cannot be prostituted and sold in bunches, like spinach or "fortunes," without becoming nothing but evil suggestion. Many of the evil things that "come true" are the result of suggestion passed on to the subject by the fortune teller. And it is interesting to note how much easier it is to remember the evil things and how they persist in returning to memory. That is because evil is more real and more omnipotent to the human thought than good.

We are warned about consulting those with a "familiar spirit" and are told that it is an abomination to the Lord. What Lord? *Your* Lord, the Father within you. The moment you take your reliance from your inner Lord and place it on another, you are abominating that power and will pay accordingly in time of need. Anytime you discount the Lord within you and place the power of life and death in another, at that moment you are becoming an abomination to the Lord within you. You have deprived Him of His expression. You have gone "a whoring after other gods."

I have consulted and interviewed *prophets* the world over, from the highest so-called scientific prophet to the lowest fortune teller on the other side of the tracks, and have found that many are called but few chosen. The percentage is low.

The almost complete failure of the prophets to tell the outcome of the war has driven them into a place of refuge, and they will not commit themselves anymore. The prophecies they give regarding this catastrophe are so nebulous as to be meaningless, and your guess is as good as mine is about the sum total. Do you know how many dates and how many terrible and fearful things have been predicted for the demise of Hitler? And the same thing was true of the old Kaiser in the former war. Yet there is the gift of prophecy, definitely one of the gifts that Jesus possessed, which enabled Him to tell the woman at the well—and so can you.

Yes, "Where there be prophecy, it shall fail." So it must be mutable and not fixed, and the way to clear the consciousness of false prophecies and fears is to look a little further in the above quotation: "But love never faileth." That is something on which you can get your stance. *Never* is a real word. There are no halfway measures about it.

Do you believe? Well, then, it is time you took a running jump and landed right into the middle of this Love of God—here, there, and everywhere, that glorious presence of God in everything and through everything and instantly able to disseminate and disintegrate every evil congestion of human thought from whatever cause. Relax into the Love of God and experience the perfect, fearless state of mind. "Perfect love casteth out fear," and out goes the fear of the evil prophecy or the old human fate patterns that have been keeping you in the hellhole of despair for years.

So "if you be in the Spirit, you are no more under the curse of the law." The curse of the law is the evil human fate. There is nothing the matter with the law; it is the curse of it which is evil, and the curse of it is the old belief in the cause and effect of the human mind. In the Christ-Consciousness, where it is consummated "before you ask," this curse of the law is wiped out. On the three-dimensional plane of human thinking, you are more or less under this curse all the time. No wonder Jesus invited you to "come unto me and be saved." Come unto the consciousness of your Permanent Identity and be saved from the karmic patterns of the congested human thought. "As for man, his days are few and filled with trouble." That is what Jesus came to help you to escape.

I have heard a dozen prophets interpret Nostradamus. These original prophecies written in now archaic French have been stretched to fit every and any situation that comes on the horizon. The English have made them fit England; the Germans,

Germany, etc., etc., and each one declares and can "prove" that he is exactly right. And so with the pyramids. Half a dozen different interpretations are about, all purporting to translate the various stones, measurements, etc. And one is appalled at one day's radio broadcast giving the various interpretations of the book of Revelation.

So what? Well, what? Go from one fortune teller to another and see how many of them agree. "I sees what I sees, and I hears what I hears, and I draws my own *delusions.*"

"Turn ye even unto me, and ye shall find rest for your souls."

> "Where there be prophecy,
> it shall fail ..."
> but "love never faileth,"
> and *never* is a long, long time.

Chapter XXII

Hid with Christ in God

"You are hid with Christ in God," and that is a better hiding place than a bomb shelter when you know what the Jesus Christ Consciousness is. And that does not disparage the bomb cellars and their use or make light of any and all intelligent cooperation with the law, but it does not keep you from knowing the hiding place that you have with you always. You may not always be within distance of a material shelter, but just the same, you have your hiding place, and when you begin to *know* this, a more definite fearlessness comes to you which enables you in turn to act wisely and intelligently. There are the "six cities of refuge" into which you may run, even though you are in a place of physical desolation; but all this is the gift of God and must be appropriated by the radical and actual belief in Him "whom to know aright is life eternal."

"Hid with Christ in God" is not hid with Jesus, as many people think. They imagine if they are repeating the words of Jesus and praising Him they will find this shelter; and while I do not deny the virtue of this practice, yet I know that the real being "hid with Christ in God" is an actual entering into the consciousness "which was also in Christ Jesus," an entering into your God-heritage and the acceptance of the Word of God as something more than letters on a printed page.

"Enter in and be saved." A lady who was very nervous and fearful about being bombed, although she lived in a remote section of the world, said, "Well, you can have your Consciousness; give me a good old bombproof cellar. It must be pretty drafty out there in Consciousness when a raid is on." So the ignorant human mind continues to measure everything by the human limitations "through the glass, darkly." She was right as far as her world went.

> But you—well, *you* are hid
> with Christ in God.
> Do you hear?
> Are you afraid?

Chapter XXIII

Between Two Opinions How Long Halt Ye?

Elijah the Prophet said unto the people:

"How long halt ye between two opinions? If the Lord be God, follow him; but if Baal, then follow him."

It is recorded, "But the people answered him not a word."

The reason they answered *not a word* is that they were afraid to "choose ye this day." They did not *believe* within their hearts. They were traveling the hellish path of indecision, believing that the Lord is one and then having altars to ten thousand household gods and beliefs.

Indecision is a sure poison which will slowly consume every bit of life, joy, and vitality from the temple. The *gesture* which causes a miracle to take place is *decision*. The "stretch forth thy hand" is made at the point of decision against every established belief in a power opposed to God. The convulsing question of Elijah struck the people dumb.

"How long halt ye between two opinions?" Why will you continue to get caught in the vise of two beliefs? If you believe God can heal you, you are through looking to other devices and people for help. When you are through, you are *through*, and you are at the point of "though he slay me, yet will I trust in him."

Between the two opinions—in other words, taking thought of the how, why, when, and where, to the action of stretching forth the hand and the making of the gesture—lies the vast and wonderful consciousness of God. Choose ye *this* day (that is today) whom ye shall serve. And then, "having done all, stand ... and see the salvation of the Lord." "If God be God, then follow him."

Stop shadow boxing. It leads nowhere. No prize fighter imagines he is going to defeat the shadow which he himself is casting, yet the human mind shadow boxes with the self-created images of disease and tries to defeat the opponent which is within and which is casting the shadow.

Stop fighting with things, people, conditions, and places and go *within* and *see* where the change takes place. "For there is nothing hid which shall not be manifested." Are you going to stand, or are you still shaking with fear and doubt?

> "And Elijah said unto the people: I, even I only, remain a prophet of the Lord; But Baal's prophets are four hundred and fifty men."

When we begin to understand the *One*, as contrasted against the *more than one*, we see the Way instead of the ways and the Power instead of the thousand and one devices of pseudo-power to make demonstrations by personal pleading or equations, systems, or personal teachings.

When the test of actual ability comes, it is always the same story. There is much talk about the power to heal, to prosper, to bring happiness for a price. The results are so pitifully lacking, and the excuses are so great. It is refreshing, at least, to see Elijah exposing this pseudo-power. He invites the believers in two powers to prepare an altar and to kill two bullocks and lay them thereon and then call upon their god or gods to set fire to the offering, saying that he will do likewise.

When all this detail had been carried out, Elijah said, "Call upon the name of your gods and put no fire under." And so the priests of Baal began to pour out a hecatomb of words, affirmations, and prayers to their gods. And Elijah, having a well-developed sense of humor, said unto them:

> "Cry aloud: for he is a god; either he is talking, or he is pursuing, or he is in a journey, or peradventure he sleepeth, and must be awaked."

He is uncovering the personal god, made in the image and likeness of man, with all the emotional flavor of the human mind.

And so, as the story goes, they went through their bag of tricks. They cut themselves; they chanted; they prophesied. In other words, they tried every maneuver of the human thought. Still nothing happened. It is interesting to watch the human thought trying to manhandle God.

Then Elijah laid his offering on the altar, digging a trench about it which he filled with water after having drenched the offering and the wood thereof with it. And not being satisfied with this complete challenge to the human thought and its belief in physics, he insisted they go through the whole thing again, drenching the altar anew with four barrels of water. Then he *prayed*—and *then* it happened. The fire descended, consumed the burnt offering, licked up the water in the trench thereabout.

The symbology of the Bible is wonderful. The illustrations therein are drastic in their treatment. There are no half measures. It is either all or nothing, and so is it with the man who makes his decision and stands by the *one* God instead of following some of the four hundred and fifty different priests of Baal. All their combined affirmations and systems will not strike a spark of fire. There is nothing within them which will set the fires. One system after another comes and wanes, proclaimed as the only. You have seen this.

This dramatic story seems vastly outside the precincts of man, but the amazing part of it is that the same power delineated in the illustration is that which passed through *you* into manifestation, just as it passed through Elijah. *Only believe*, said the Master, and presently this *only* begins to sink in and become active.

Yes, even the water in the trench was licked up; every supposed law of physics is set at naught. Everybody knows it is foolishness to expect to cure an incurable disease. It is all right to talk about the cure of such things, but when you are faced with it, then what?

How about moving over a space or two into the dimension of the power operating through Elijah, where the appearances were put to naught and the fires burned the offering, wet though it was.

Do you believe? I am speaking to *you*. Or are you trying to make God do your bidding as did the disciples of Baal?

> "For God sent not his Son into the world to condemn the world; but that the world through him might be saved."

The *only reason* of Jesus was to set aside the fate patterns established by the priests of Baal and to put at naught all their findings and learnings. God does not ask that conditions be right. When He is called upon, He answers more surely than an electric switch when touched. To suppose you can demonstrate this power as a side issue in life is to experience the fruits of ignorance.

> The only fires that can burn you are those set by yourself (Homer).

Eventually, you *see* and discover yourself, the Son of God, perfect and eternal.

"But we all, with open face beholding as in a glass the glory of the Lord, are changed into the same image from glory to glory ... ."

Do you *hear* what it says?—"... are changed (Do you follow Me?) into the same (identical) image."

Can you begin to *feel*—believe? Or will you run to a priest of Baal and seek a way and means of demonstrating this already established fact?

As the road sign is invisible at night until the light of your car is turned upon it, so is the love of God invisible until the recognition is made. The love of God is always present, as are the road signs, but without recognition apparently invisible. The healing power of Jesus Christ does not take place until acknowledgement of its existence is made. "Believest thou that I am able to do this unto thee?"

There is a hearing through the nonhearing. When God speaks, it is in a "still small voice" and is *inaudible* until recognized.

Chapter XXIV

Symbols

There is the shepherd, tending the flocks by night—night on the desert, the heavens pulsating with stars. His meditation wraps about him as does his burnoose. A faithful dog lies at his feet; he rests on his staff and contemplates the beauty of life.

Then there is the shepherd who, leaving his sheep, goes over the rough mountain ways searching for the lost lamb and rejoicing when he finds it.

And the one who leads beside still waters and through green pastures with the steadying assurance of his rod and staff.

And yet another, with tenderness leading those with young, gently carrying the lamb in his bosom.

Yes, the shepherd is something beautiful to contemplate, with the calm, steady flow of his unruffled consciousness as he stands guard over his flock.

One day I was idling about in a canoe on a beautiful little lake in northern Germany. The day was perfect; the lake, a mill pond, just beginning to be burnished by the setting sun. An apple orchard was billowing in pink-white loveliness. Fresh green grass ran like liquid paint over the hills, Pan dashing in and out of the bushes setting them aflame. On the horizon a relaxed windmill was slowly coming to the end of its day's work. And there on the hilltop stood a shepherd, leaning on his crook, while his flock was huddled about him. Suddenly I saw *my symbol* and paddled the slim canoe in that direction.

When I came up to him, he was standing with his eyes closed. I startled him! He was a likely type of shepherd, with large blue eyes and a bronzed skin. A heavy thatch of blond hair, sunburned into gold, cropped from under a torn hat. A perfect specimen.

After a few inanities of opening conversation, I edged carefully toward my subject. I wanted to find out some of the deep meditations that were going through his mind. And finally taking a headlong plunge, I said to him, "And what do you think about all day as you stand here tending your sheep?"

He eyed me for a moment and then said in a gruff voice, "Well, sometimes I think about what the old woman is going to have for supper, and sometimes I don't think about nothing."

With that statement he knocked my whole category of shepherds to bits. They lay in a heap of disillusionment at my feet. I left my shepherd and paddled home. The sun was really setting now, and the lake was amethyst, my heart the same color.

When I turned in through the gate, the old gardener was talking to his much indulged cat. "Ah, no, Bizzel, you are a fake. You do not catch mice. You sleep and eat my food; you pose as a mouse

That Ye Might Have

catcher, but you are nothing but a figure, a symbol. And so I get some traps, lazy one."

The power, then, was not in the thing; it was the consciousness back of it since its value could be changed by the slightest whim of man.

Luck was not in the four-leafed clover, a horseshoe, but in the mind of the man. Healing was not in the body of Jesus but in the consciousness that *believed*.

The consciousness of reality could and would project thousands of symbols, which would react toward one in a positive way when he saw *through* the symbol and into the consciousness back of it.

> The consciousness of anything carries with it the ability to project its symbols anywhere, at any time.

No matter how many shepherds fell by the wayside, the consciousness of what they stood for could and would reproduce the symbol at any time.

Within the *Word* is the power of fulfillment. Thus, when the admonition "go into all the world" is spoken from consciousness, it brings with it all the means of fulfillment and completion. Yet it remains a printed word on the pages of thousands of books. Examination of the printed pages results in defeat, for the power is not there.

A million litanies and prayers, lacking consciousness, will heal nothing. "Open your eyes" is no more efficacious than "one, two, three, four" unless there is the consciousness of Light back of it.

If there be that consciousness, then the words fulfill themselves with a lightning rapidity which beggars all effort, thought, or reason. The Word becoming flesh is the Word back of the symbol. The Word of Life will embody Its symbol of health, and that health will remain as long as the mind is stayed on *that* consciousness.

Health is merely the symbol or out-picturing of Life. Jesus said plainly, "I am the life," and the consciousness of this causes the symbol of health to automatically take shape and form, and "by a way ye know not of." It is beyond all human reason or belief; past finding out as far as the human thinking is concerned. The human effort to make things happen, to heal or cure, is like planting a post and expecting it to grow into a tree. The same action might have planted a tree. Both operations are the same, but one is alive and grows and expands into fruition, while the other is dead and rots.

"Who did hinder ye, that ye did not obey the truth?" Why did ye obey a man and not Me? Why were you not healed, when you went through all the motions of healing? You had treatments by the dozens.

As surely as the contemplation of God as universal and perfect produces gold in a fish's mouth, thereby setting aside all the wisdom of man, so does the Permanent Identity (the Christ in you) recognize this verity and releases the manifestation, or symbol, in the temple (body) of Jesus (John Smith).

That Ye Might Have

"Behold, I come quickly, and my reward is with me." The Consciousness, once recognized, comes into manifestation quickly, rendering asunder the veils of human belief and exposing the perfect manifestation. If you have ever wondered why Jesus counseled you, "Buy of me gold tried in the fire, that thou mayest be rich; and white raiment, that thou mayest be clothed," you will now understand why you are being led away from the symbol and back to the Consciousness, which is the real substance. That is the only gold worthy of your contemplation—the substance which can and does cast its symbol of the thing necessary at the precise moment. The worthlessness of the dollar in a desert proves the worthlessness of the symbol, but bread and water would be another story.

Unto *you* is given to know the mysteries! Anything is possible to God, and so to you—*anything* that you can and do accept *in consciousness*.

"The Lord is my shepherd; I shall not want," and He springs into being in your Soul, even at the sight of the gruff young man standing atop a German hillock.

Meditations

Not a Sparrow Falleth

Recently, in Los Angeles, a lady passed away, leaving her pet dog a house, a car with services of a chauffeur, money for food, and orders for two special chicken dinners a week.

Many who read it laughed; some thought it shameful; some shed a tear over the half-tragic thing. But some saw the great heart of Love which was trying with all its human power to reach out into the future and protect the thing it loved and perhaps the only thing which had ever returned that Love.

When I read it, I suddenly had such a *near* feeling of the Love of God, the desire of the Creator towards His creation. "Oh, Jerusalem, Jerusalem, how often would I have taken you to my breast, as a hen gathereth her chickens under her wings ... ." How the love of God is pressing upon the diaphragm of your mind, knocking at the door, waiting for man to awaken from his dream of evil and let Him in to break bread with him.

Suddenly it was as if the great wings of Love had over-shadowed me and I was hugged close to the very soul of it all. Many have talked of the Love of God, but it was such an abstract quality it was worthless; but suddenly, through the awakened consciousness, I knew that we should actually, literally, "call no man your Father." I understood why Jesus was so sure of Himself; why He could call upon

His Father—because the Father was only waiting for a chance to express His Love through Him.

All the fear ran out of me like sand running through an hourglass, and the warmth of this Love that is "past all (human thought-taking) understanding" filled me with warm pulsating Life—the Presence.

"Not a sparrow falleth ... ." Not a thing takes place which is not known. The only reason something isn't done about it is because there is no conscious contact established between man and God. We are so afraid of it all because through the thought-taking mind it has been nothing but words.

Yet everybody is the body of God and is the place where His Love can and will express. When the understanding of this takes place, "the lion shall lie down with the lamb." All the evil propensities of the human thought will be dissipated and gone.

The little lady in Los Angeles poured out her love on the thing that opened the channel to receive it, and Jesus asked this pertinent question of you: "If ye then, being evil, know how to give good gifts unto your children, how much more shall your Father who is in heaven give good things unto them that ask him?"

Do you see that "heretofore ye have asked for nothing"? *Now* ask, "that your joy might be full."

Do you begin to understand why your heart has been full of fear and evil forebodings? And do you also begin to experience the warm surge of Love

That Ye Might Have

which is flowing, constantly flowing from God to His manifestation?

"He careth for you." Not maybe or perhaps. Do you hear? Do you believe in the new Light of the no-thought consciousness, in the pure recognition of the Presence, and are you beginning to feel the heavenly relaxation which causes you to know that it is well with thee? All the worries, cares, and troubles, all the unsolved things, and the past evils are buried in this sea of Love, the Love which casteth out fear.

"If thou knewest the gift of God ...." If you would only sense-feel this Love of God and suddenly let it sweep you out of the mental miasma of beliefs, you would find yourself in heaven here and now.

Beloved!
Watch with me one hour
on this Love of God.

Adultery

In a recent exposé on the Aramaic language, which, as you know, is the language of Jesus, one finds the word *adultery* has largely to do with pregnancy, that the real adultery was the act of copulation after conception had taken place. This, of course, does not in any sense invite license.

We know that all prayer that is made in consciousness is answered. The moment it is made, the conception takes place, and after that the duration of the gestation is entirely out of the hands of the one making the prayer.

Sometimes it may be instantly that the conception takes and a body is set on earth; sometimes it may travel a longer route, in which time *you* are being prepared, if you but knew it, to receive the new idea that is coming into your earth, which is going to change the face of everything.

"Be not like the heathens, for they think with much repetition to gain the ear of God; but when you pray ... ." The insistence of trying to re-create after the conception has taken place shows the entire disregard for the principle and shows the lack of actual *belief* in God and is the committing of adultery against which we are warned.

All this wonderful symbology which takes place when the Word of God gives up Its meaning will fill you with joy, for eventually you will stop the adulterous habit of praying and acknowledging that it is done, only to go back again and again to the proposition and try again to re-create it.

Once the conception has taken place, the mysteries surrounding the birth of the new idea are shielded from human eye or thought. "I have a way ye know not of," and it is never twice the same. That is why no formulae will work and no set idea will ever come into being.

Stop the adultery. Make an end to praying. Stand and see the salvation of the Lord.

Stop adulterating the Word of God with the words of man. Stop adulterating everything spiritual with a concession that it is necessary to go through evil to get good. Stop this adultery in prayer.

"Thou shalt not commit adultery."

Preparation

Despise not the chastening of the Lord.

So often we start kicking against appearances which we are unable to move by our best work. Later, after we have virtually worn ourselves out fretting through a thousand and one excuses of the human mind, we have found we have been held in that place awaiting the new expression. We have been held many times in what seemed a meaningless place, doing what appeared to be meaningless things, to discover later we were being prepared for the next expression.

When you have made your prayer, when you have made an end to it, the answer is forthcoming, and that answer must be seen in its right light to be understood. It is wonderful when you begin to perceive this. "I shall stand upon my watch, and see what the Lord has to say unto me."

"Wait patiently for him … and he shall bring it to pass." But many times, much must transpire on the outside before you are ready to step into the new expression. If you crash through the shell that has seemed a bondage, before it gives way by the divine impulsion, you may find you are unable to stand or understand the next move. All the time you are held against your human will, you later discover, is time of preparation. "Not my will, but thine be done," and the lovely relaxation in God with "Lord, what

That Ye Might Have

will You have me to do?" It is all so glorious when you stop kicking against the pricks and let something take place naturally. You are being *prepared*.
    Watch, you know not
at what moment *I* come.

The Gods Give Thread

I recall a lovely quotation which goes somewhat after this manner: "The gods give thread to those who start a web." This is not verbatim, but the substance of it is there.

The moment you *arise* in consciousness to the recognition of the Father, at that moment He moves towards you with the robe, ring, etc. The moment you start *pouring* the oil, the three drops become unlimited, and the moment you *recognize* the Presence, the handful of meal becomes unlimited.

The web, which may be very elaborate, is started with a tiny bit of substance. When you discover it within you, you are like unto the spider that manufactures his thread as fast as he uses it and *only* as he uses it. So go ahead and weave your pattern; there is always enough to accomplish the perfect pattern if you will go ahead.

>Yes, "the gods give thread
>to those who start a web."
>Ponder this a while.

Fire and Duck

The story is told of a small detachment of men who got lost from their company during maneuvers and were marching along in echelon when they were discovered by their enemy, who thought to surround them by forming a U-formation about them. The leader of the detachment discovered what had happened, and as soon as the enemy had had time to take its position, he gave the command to "fire and take cover," which was done. The enemy immediately returned fire, shooting most of their own men across the intervening space, thereby making it possible for the detachment to escape unharmed.

This illustration reminded me of the way of Jesus. After the Word had been spoken, He retired from the appearances and let the evil illusion take care of its own destruction. In the vernacular of the army: "Fire and duck." Speak the Word and retire to a place of quiet.

> See that you tell no man; get out of the way; let the thing which has been so powerful destroy itself. It is wonderful!

Notes

The instant you become conscious—*really conscious*—of a thing, you possess it. The consciousness and the thing are one in reality, and the unseen takes body and form from this recognition.

The instant you believe—actually *believe*—you stop thinking *of* and *about*. Belief is actually acceptance. The "thought-push" stops; there is a relaxation, a letting go, and this very Divine Indifference makes it possible for the "impossible" thing to happen.

Once we are hypnotized to appearances, there is nothing in human thought that will break the spell. Like the bird and the serpent is man with an incurable disease. Though he, like the bird, has means of escape, yet he is so fixed on what he sees or hears that he becomes immovable. Judging from appearances causes one to become static.

༄ ༄

Until you can see God in the devil, you cannot see God. Do you still believe that God is *All*? This ability to *see* God in the apparent evil is what causes the evaporation of the evil coating of human thought, which has obscured the Golden Being.

In the jungle, the voodoo priest claims power to reanimate dead bodies so that soulless men operate on the earth and are being directed by a master mind. Whether this is true or a theory, it is interesting how much of it is attempted today. Many reanimate dead pictures of evil and cause them to live again. They fear modern-day zombies as much as the most cringing savage under the spell of the tom-tom.

Just recently, an intelligent man came to me crying because someone was doing what he called "malpracticing." He explained that malpractice was an evil function he had learned about which worked all sorts of ills but which *did not exist*. He was chased about by a zombie which existed *only* in his own mind. This zombie of belief was backed by thousands of testimonies of intelligent people but was violently denied.

Anything you violently deny "exists" for you as a reality, with the strength, the intensity of your denial. Your zombie pursues you like your shadow. It is part and parcel of *you,* projected by you and sustained by you. The moment it is out of *your* mind, it is out of the only place it ever existed.

Remembering the deep sleep that fell upon Adam, we begin to see that he is still dreaming some of the imagination he took upon himself when he decided to co-create with God in a universe that was already completed.

Abraham was accounted one of the strongholds of truth, and we see what was back of the tremendous power he was able to wield. "Abraham believed God, and it was counted unto him for righteousness." When you *believe* and stop trying to believe for the purpose of personal gain, then it is *accounted* unto you as righteousness. Remember that the man who has righteousness in his heart can never (has neither the need nor capacity to) beg bread. "I have never seen the righteous begging bread." Wonderful, isn't it?

Through recognition of the One—here, there, everywhere—we begin to experience It. It should not be difficult to see God in action and manifestation. Why should it be so difficult to experience Him, Life in the midst of you, as an actuality and not as something called health, which is at the mercy of human thought?

Jesus made His recognition and could enter into a *oneness* with God. So we, reflecting as in a mirror the glory of God, are changed into the *same* image. We see the gradual merging of Jesus (matter) with the Christ (Spirit) producing literally the flesh, in which we can *see* God. What we see from this elevation is reality and not the shadow of a reflection any longer.

"My eyes have seen the glory of the Lord." Your eyes actually experience the vision, and you exclaim, "Whereas before I was blind, now (at this instant) I can see." This state of consciousness will literally heal the blind, but this cannot be tried, worked, or demonstrated—it is the assumption of consciousness. How can you assume anything if you do not first know that it exists as a reality?

Jesus achieved non-action in action. He did nothing, yet everything changed. The picture shown to Him on the Mount became visible to those present. Nothing took place; something was revealed.

>So is it when you,
>the Golden One,
>know the ways of Life.

About the Author

Walter Lanyon was highly respected as a spiritual teacher of Truth. He traveled and lectured to capacity crowds all over the world, basing his lectures, as he said, "solely on the revelation of Jesus Christ."

At one point, he underwent a profound spiritual awakening, in which he felt "plain dumb with the wonder of the revelation." This enlightening experience "was enough to change everything in my life and open the doors of the Heaven that Jesus spoke of as here and now. I know what it was. I lost my personality; it fell off of me like an old rag. It just wasn't the same anymore."

His prolific writings continue to be sought out for their timeless message, put forth in a simple, direct manner, and they have much to offer serious spiritual seekers.

Walter Clemow Lanyon was born in the U.S. on October 27, 1887, and he passed away in California on July 4, 1967.

Printed in Great Britain
by Amazon